Listen
to your
Garden

HIDDEN DIMENSIONS

Jim Warren

◆ FriesenPress

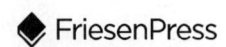

Suite 300 - 990 Fort St
Victoria, BC, V8V 3K2
Canada

www.friesenpress.com

Copyright © 2016 by Jim Warren
First Edition — 2016

All rights reserved.

No part of this publication may be reproduced in any form, or by any means, electronic or mechanical, including photocopying, recording, or any information browsing, storage, or retrieval system, without permission in writing from FriesenPress.

ISBN
978-1-4602-9652-3 (Hardcover)
978-1-4602-9653-0 (Paperback)
978-1-4602-9654-7 (eBook)

1. BIOGRAPHY & AUTOBIOGRAPHY, PERSONAL MEMOIRS

Distributed to the trade by The Ingram Book Company

Table of Contents

Forward... vii
Point and Counterpoint 1
Ruminants 2
The Extraordinary Ordinary 4
Cost of Leisure.....................................5
Shed Seaweed......................................7
CawCawphony 9
Bee Bumbling.....................................11
Eagle Trial..13
Dr. Flower..14
The Scion...16
The Thicket.......................................18
Evergreen Magnolia..............................19
A So-called Lawn 21
Dahlia Indigestion 23
Houseplant Jungle 25
Heather and Heath...............................27
Rototill Your Compost Pile......................28
Learning from Bad Examples 30
Ambivalence.....................................31
Hedge trimmer 33
Community Vegetable Garden 35
The Fraser River Delta 36
The Four Elements...............................37
Birdbrain...38
The Motley Crew 40
The Pansy..41
Deer Damage Coping............................42
Snow load..44

Prepared for Snow	45
Whitewash Cover-up	46
Eagle Attack	47
Shred and Burn	48
Sex in the Island	49
Gladiolus and Mums	51
Impetuous Gardening	53
The Golden Apple; Quince	54
Unnatural Act	55
Peripheral Vision	57
Sex in the Greenhouse	58
Birdie Num Nums	60
Blueberry Nets	62
Doomed	64
Canada Geese and Black Aphids	65
Raspberry and Pea pickin'	67
Mouse	69
The California Quail	71
The Grinches and the Olympic Flame	72
The Tortoise and the Hare	73
Fauna Change	74
Homemade Wine	76
The Mixed Hedgerow	77
Mother Nature's Fruits	78
Agonal Bloom	80
Heritage Dahlia	82
African Violets	84
Sunrise Lost	85
The Altar Guild	87
The Green Tree Frog	88
The Scythe	89
Slugs	91

The Botanist	93
Currants	95
Cherry Pie	97
Loganberries	99
Robin, Canadian of Course	101
Osprey	103
Rhubarb, the First Fruit	104
Squirrel Scraps	106
Clam Digging	108
Garden Bones	110
Cucumbers	112
Witching	114
Mother Nature's Garden	116
Gumbo Soil	118
Golden Bantam Corn	119
Bee Keeping	120
Powerless in Paradise	122
Mold	124
Homegrown Vegetables	125
Pee on Your Compost	127
Crum Jelly	128
The Church Bazaar	129
The Wet Coast	131
Winter moon	132
Peony Leaves	133
Garden Party	134
Harrow my Roadway	136
Pruneophobia	138
First Nation's Spirit	140
Maple Pole Bean Mania	141
The Three Sisters	143
Apple Surplus	145

The Past is not a Foreign Country	146
Fall Season	148
The Exhibitor	150
Tree Crop Failure	152
Weeding and Squatting	153
The lady and the Gardener	154
Random Width Siding	155
Crow World Revisited	157
Dinosaur Rhubarb	159
Beach Walk	160
Bee Cradle	161
Organic Food	162
Michaelmas	164
Bad Ideas	166
The Fertile Mind	168
Turf the Old	169
Lotus Island Spring	171
Formication and Slug Fest	173
Dormant Spray	175
The Un-heavenly Host	177
Tent Caterpillar Egg Cases	179
Tent Caterpillar Moths	181
Scatological Investigations	183
Lilacs	185
Grass is a Plant	187
Gunnera Attacked	189
Penny for your Plots	191
Winter Ducks	193
Black Bamboo	195
Regal Gooseberry Jam	197
Quince Jelly	199
Identity, Our Tool is Us	201

Forward

I wondered about repackaging old essays I had written about gardens in prior publications. FriesenPress had suggested I do so, producing a garden book. There can't be a better reason for producing things twice than providing an opportunity twice. My garden essays had been mixed in with random essays of a general nature, so for those readers whose interest is particularly pricked by reading about gardening of a somewhat offbeat nature, you are my kind of people and I hope you will forgive me for repeating myself.

When I define listening to the garden it is not only hearing sounds, the sole responsibility of the auditory branch of the eighth cranial nerve; it is sensing with all the seven senses that we are blessed with. This is the sort of listening that is much broader than hearing and tells us we can be successful if we can translate the lesson. The lesson has to do with us and not the garden per se. There is little in these essays to satisfy the gardener who requires a menu of information. I don't consider myself an expert in gardening. There are plenty of professionals in horticulture whose knowledge and love of the subject is available. They could be master gardeners. They could be hired hands. Amazon lists 18,400 gardening titles available today so there is no shortage of expert instruction in gardening. There is probably no shortage of titles referring to looking at the garden, but they don't list any that advocate listening to the garden that I can determine.

One may legitimately ask, "How can the garden help me grow?" There could be much that will satisfy those who require understanding of a sort that fulfills Aristotle's observation, "Nature does nothing in vain." I suppose he could be inferring that our growth under Nature's tutelage will not be in vain. In the garden we live with inhabitants that are rooted, some who scamper, and some who flutter. We have to figure out what they need. Since we are one with them all, they need what we need.

If you think this is a touch of madness you can read on to the 18,400 titles to show Mother Nature that you are the boss. To listen, however, one needs all seven senses. I will tell you what these senses are if you read the book carefully.

In the meantime, if someone writes an overly long foreword, putative readers can rightly ask, when do we get to eat?

Point and Counterpoint

Years ago, while working in the orchard pruning apple trees and sitting by a tree trunk taking a breather, I saw Gramps, the pianist's father, walking up the road beside the orchard on my right. He walked slowly and haltingly because he was breathless from an advanced lung cancer, but he was still in good spirits and mining all he could from the seams of his remaining life. We could have set to music and orchestrated with some sort of cadence his gait and surreptitious appearance. He had emerged from the kitchen door on the right of the cottage, closed it quietly, and had a location in mind. As I watched and thought about him and his life ebbing away after so many years I still saw spirit and desire. I knew he was going up the road for a smoke. There was a flash of movement on the path on the left side of the cottage. The sliding door opened and closed silently and fourteen-year-old Ruth, my daughter, emerged, ostensibly unnoticed, and quietly walked up the pathway on the left side of the orchard, clearly on her way to have a forbidden smoke. She had spirit and desire and was going to try everything, childhood ebbing away. As they proceeded apace, unknown to one another and known by me in silence, I saw this as a drama, a point and counterpoint, interdependent harmonically yet independent in rhythm and contour. Three players engaged in a small rhythm of life.

Ruminants

Yesterday, when I looked out the window on Lotus Island, I said to the pianist, "Look, there is a doe and a yearling lying on our footpath, chewing their cud!" Their front legs were crossed in complete repose, a posture not adapted to rapid takeoff. They stayed on the path for a good part of the afternoon. It's safe here! I guess in another place and time they, and all the other Class Ruminantia, for that matter, were often surrounded by predators. Mother Nature demanded rapid food gathering by her ruminants in sites of danger. They had to always be alert and ready to flee; only later would they have a chance to regurgitate and break down the snatched food at leisure in found safety and sanctuary. I ask myself from time to time why I would write about trivial matters such as two deer relaxing in a sanctuary of sorts when the world is going through such monumental events (war, revolution, economic fears, shaken faith, individuals on the cusp of disaster). And here I am today, ruminating along with my deer. Chewing snatched cud of information and ideas, pulled rapidly from the trees of knowledge, gathered in a hurry, and not fully digested! Much of that information was gathered during the momentum of a hurried life, in which I was feeding quickly. I guess, to answer my own question, I am writing for myself, in part, and it is not trivial! I should really call it "reflection" since the psychiatrists unfortunately have now tainted "rumination." It's nothing more than having a good chew at material that you bring up, in order to break it down again. In a sea of troubles, we have to reach for a plank to stop ourselves from drowning. We have to float! I guess my plank in life is to celebrate the ordinary stuff of existence that may give some buoyancy. Age gives one time to ruminate/reflect on information gathered in a hurry. Now I can repose with my legs crossed and let go!

The Extraordinary Ordinary

When Esther Summerson* ventured out after months of a completely confining illness—smallpox—a deadly disease as it was then, before Edward Jenner's discovery of the vaccine, she spoke for Dickens and for all of us about the realized world around us. As she looked from the carriage for the first time in months, she said, "I found every breath of air, and every scent and every flower and leaf and blade of grass, and every passing cloud, and everything in nature, more beautiful and wonderful to me than I had ever found it yet. This was my first gain from my illness." Dickens has encapsulated in four lines the content and the expression of the healing nature of the garden. To emerge into the light from whatever dark night of the soul you have been confined to is a revelation that the ordinary is truly extraordinary. To merge your streams of consciousness and unconsciousness with the streams of Mother Nature, seen and unseen, heard and felt and smelled! The profound, once experienced, is enough! To expect it again is greedy. To have it always would render it powerless. The lasting gain is not in the exultation but in the serenity.

* Ester Summerson, from *Bleak House* (by Charles Dickens)

Cost of Leisure

I read somewhere of a French gentleman, living on the beachfront in Normandy, who required his children and grandchildren to bring back a sack of seaweed for his garden each time they went to the beach. No pleasure without accompanying industry. It was not declared in the article that he compelled his friends to do likewise! Had he done so, it is possible that he would have ended up having few friends as well as progressively indifferent offspring. Over the years, I had taken a leaf from this man's book and endeavoured where possible, but only for myself, never to take or do something to the right of me at point B without doubling up by bringing something back or doing something to the left of me at point A. Work on the way down and work of a new nature on the way back, or leisure on the way down and leisure on the way back, or a combination of both! Trying to never waste a moment, either at play or work! Programming!

Wasted moments and leisure may have much more in common than we realize. One of the things they have in common is that they are often both derided by those who have little of either! Work and play may have much more in common for the fortunate, who may not be able to differentiate between them. I wish I had composted the Frenchman's leaf in my earlier days rather than seeing it as an opportunity. Now that I am older, that A and B programme doesn't work for me any longer. I can't judge but I suspect that a happy balance through life, a willingness not to impose your values on others, and striving to work at the things you love is the fortunate choice. Live for the present, not the future. If you do it well the future will take care of itself. Applying this balance gives autonomy to you and everyone you love! There is no way that I was a gentleman or that this was Normandy. I may have been dumb enough to engage in A and B for a while but I didn't contaminate my children or grandchildren with my compulsions. I left them to follow their own.

Shed Seaweed

My son-in-law and I were sitting on a beach log this afternoon and the tide was coming in with a strong onshore wind and moderate wave action in the harbour. For the past two weeks there had been a large accumulation of shed sea lettuce and sundry other seaweed carried in by the tidal action. There is a lot of lateral tide movement on our beach as well, and the accessible part of the beach that welcomes and retains the weed is about five hundred feet long. After a few days, as the high tide lowers, the weed tossed up on the beach dries and loses some of its salinity and its definition. In the olden days, I used to collect much of this material for compost and top dressing.

The ocean gives up its sea lettuce in August and its eelgrass in October, both of them gifted to those who scavenge the shore for that kind of treasure. I have always had a fantasy that if I had a donkey hitched to a large two-wheeled cart I could walk the shore and pitchfork the drying weed into my cart with a lot more ease than trying to haul it up my twelve steps from the beach in a garbage pail. In the distant past, my Irish ancestors used this gift of seaweed to create soil on barren stony headlands. This was where they were banished to from the fertile valley lands usurped from them. As we sat together on the log and looked reflectively at the drying weed, I thought aloud, "The line of drying weed above the tidemark is evenly ten feet wide now. Over the five-hundred-foot length it averages two inches thick. By my calculation that is 833.3 cubic feet of loose compost from that little area." What the sea gives up today it will take back tomorrow unless we act! I wish I had another lifespan where my fantasy was reality and I had a donkey and cart like my headland ancestors!

CawCawphony

My neighbour has a large stand of west coast maples and cottonwoods near our property. In addition, I have holly and hawthorns near the property line. These thorn-bearing trees are safe repositories for nesting crows. The nests are well-hidden from marauders. I have an orchard with cherries and small fruits, amongst others. The crows' bedrooms, nurseries, and living rooms appear to be largely on the neighbour's property. The kitchens, dining rooms, and toilets are in western red cedar trees overlooking our deck. This seems to be fledgling time and the constant cacophony is frightful. There seems to be a crisis of ownership between the humans and the crows. The crows' kitchens also double as the toilets. A crow, after picking a juicy cherry or a small red plum in the garden, brings the fruit to the kitchen. The kitchen is a branch where some food preparation goes on: positioning the cherry or plum between the toes on the branch, tenderizing the skin, pitting, and finally swallowing. The crow's gastrocolic reflex is triggered by the meal. They appear to have a highly sensitive trigger prompting the gastrocolic event, possibly due to the shorter distance from the stomach to the rectum than yours or mine. This gastrocolic event is accompanied, dare I say, by enthusiastic crowing. Maybe even derisive! Since the favourite place to eat is the kitchen/toilet overlooking our painted deck, we are greeted with abundant guano that seems to have remarkable adherent properties. Each time I leave the house to toil in the soil, the watch bird announces my progress. If I bring my pressure washer to remove hardened and adherent guano,

I am greeted with a chorus of insults. They don't seem to care! The variety of vocalizations is remarkable. It's just they are so darned intrusive—or instead, maybe it's me.

Bee Bumbling

Wild bees had made a nest in the Styrofoam float under the seat of my rowboat. They hollowed out a home not accessible to sprays, since it was hidden from view, and they were never pleased to see a face near their home. The boat sits on a ramp down to the beach. I elected to drown them because I knew no other safe way to get rid of them. Lack of ready access prevented spraying and I didn't want to burn my boat seat if I tried to set the nest on fire. I hate doing this to bees. It's so contrary to Mother Nature's grand design. My son-in-law and I manoeuvred the boat gingerly at intervals onto the beach. We pulled it down a foot or two and then ran away when the angry bees looked around for the enemy. Pulling and scattering eventually got the boat off the ramp and onto the beach and relatively level so it could be filled completely with water. We filled the boat to above the bee's nest with water from the hose. The tide came in but thankfully it was calm.

I went down in the evening to see the results. All the daytime foragers were back, and were angry and hanging around the ramp. I couldn't ramp up the boat since it was full of water and the bees wouldn't let me near it. In securing it for a further tide I was stung and fell over on the beach trying to evade the bees. No problem! The following morning I was going to work and searched high and low for my cell phone. I phoned myself in various locations. No luck. I finally went down to the beach where I fell. There it was, lying on a pile of seaweed. It had rained that night. It was perched on seaweed indicating the high tide margin. I was sure it was trash. Then it rang. The pianist was calling me. This whole epistle sounds like an episode with the Keystone Cops at work. They always seemed to get their man the hard way! I needed to get to Lotus City quickly to do something easy like my surgical list!

Eagle Trial

This morning, looking out into the harbour at some distance, I watched two monster wings flapping with what appeared to be desperation. At first it looked like a seal. On close inspection, however, it was a mature eagle in the water trying to take off—to no avail. The pianist and I watched for about ten minutes as it intermittently flapped and struggled and got nowhere. I couldn't bear to watch any longer as I thought it was exhausting itself and soon would drown. The pianist said the same thing as we were going out to the car to leave the house. Suddenly, she said, "Look, it took off!" I looked back and it was gone. Then it hove into view in a tight circle just in front of us, close to the water, flying easily with what looked like a big bird in its talons. Not a bufflehead or a little duck, but probably a merganser, since there are a lot of them out there right now. The prey was almost too heavy for the eagle to lift off with, impaired by the half-wing swing at the water surface. If the eagle can't lift off, it can drown, as it is hard for it to detach from the prey (due to claw locking). Makes you think, doesn't it, how easy it is to bite off more than you can chew? Can't move on, can't let go, nearly going under—seduced by the big prize. Little and often, little and often!

Dr. Flower

My mum and dad in retirement lived in a high-rise rental unit in Lotus City for a number of years. There were a large number of units rented almost exclusively by elderly people. My dad, in his heyday, had grown an abundant number of dahlias and gladioli and missed the prospect of cut flowers always being available for their home. He spent half of his horticultural lifetime, as well, giving away flowers to all and sundry. It was his shtick! Since I am a chip off the old block I have grown dahlias for a number of years in some volume here on Lotus Island. I grew gladioli for a while as well but eventually quit because the deer eat the florets. They don't eat the leaves, but what is a glad without flowers? The deer here may browse a little on some of the dahlias, but not much, and then only the leaves. If they are too persistent I give the plant a spray of Plantskydd. I started taking dahlias to my parents at Lotus City once a week. They had a few friends they asked me to bring some for as well. My donations were well-received and soon most of the other renters also waited for me outside as I showed up in their parking lot at the same time every Wednesday. My "customer" base grew like wildfire and I started to use the truck to haul the plants. They called me Dr. Flower. I'm not sure that I liked the name. It sounds like Dr. Dolittle or Mr. Rogers, not an image I necessarily coveted. However, the name stuck so I had to wear it. In point of fact I loved the idea of dahlias spread throughout the apartment block. No doubt there was some ego fulfillment for me. Nothing is fully clean. The love of colour and beauty by older people in a concrete apartment made the gift-giving a continuation of my dad's generosity. It was a boon to me as well because a few days later the dahlia would have needed dead-heading so it was really little additional trouble. My dad died, my mother moved to a nursing home, my truck expired, and I ended my flower-toting activity!

The Scion

The scion is a precious plant shoot or the precious offspring of a wealthy or great family, severed from its origins and moved with care to grow with new roots. Grafting a shoot of a fine plant specimen on a hardy rootstock to propagate it widely or create a more hardy plant or one with altered shape or size makes sense. It's been done for years and horticulture as we know it could not exist without grafting. Down deep, however, it still seems to me a manipulation of Mother Nature. It's a bit hypocritical on my part to say this since my garden, like everyone else's, is full of grafted specimens. The classification of the shoot as a "scion" must come from a particular past, when the promising offspring of a great or wealthy family was "grafted" or lifted to a new setting. A successful take of a graft in the case of a plant shoot would depend on accurate matching of the cut surface cambium layer of the shoot and the root stock to which it was grafted, secure fixation for a period of time until union, and avoidance of contamination and dehydration.

This careful attention to detail was not practised by those charged with the grafting and transplanting of most people in the seventeenth and eighteenth centuries, dispersing excess populations to this shore. It was a higgledy-piggledy mix and included both the pianist's and my families of origin. There were no "scions" there! Some survived, some didn't. There was no matching of people's cambium layers so they had no organic union to rely on. There was no consideration of the right season to graft. There was no tight wrapping and waxing for fixation and protection of the graft site from movement and dehydration. There were no measures taken to avoid contamination. "Luck and pluck" were the governing principles of that transplantation and grafting. We tend to forget how much we owe our forebears. They are a national treasure, warts and all. Someone hopefully will emerge as the family librarian in each generation to retain history or herstory! Then we will augment the knowledge of from whom we are come, from where we came, and by what means we were grafted.

The Thicket

The thicket, even better the briar patch, is sanctuary for small feathered and furry friends; the denser the thicket the better! If in the well-ordered and cultivated garden there are periodic small thickets, especially near your windows, you will enjoy an abundance of creatures and also provide a measure of safety for them! Your abundance will increase since these thickets will be home and partial larder for the broody. It's unfortunate that urban dwellers may have more difficulty establishing or protecting the thicket since thickets are necessarily untidy, the briar patch even more so—and often an affront to scrupulous neighbours. Here in the rural garden on Lotus Island, Mother Nature's display of thickets blends with the efforts of the elderly eclectic gentleman. Mother Nature gardens in her own inestimable way and I in my trial-and-error fashion. The bird feeder and the birdhouse, while of some value, do not supplant the thicket or briar patch in meeting the needs of the creatures. In fact, they may foster a culture of dependency that is counterproductive to the well-being of the vulnerable. Well-meaning activity on the part of animal lovers may expose animals to more predation and disease and interfere with survival skills in an uncertain world. This applies to us as well as our fellow creatures. We hominids also need a thicket sanctuary where we can return after we venture out. We all live in an uncertain world and need to learn survival skills. Blessed assurance is that our thicket may still be there. Kindness is: come as close to Mother Nature as you dare!

Evergreen Magnolia

Smack-dab right in the middle of our view of Lotus Island harbour was our large evergreen magnolia (Magnolia grandiflora). It has been a fertile source of family interaction for years as to its origin, utility, morphology, and status. Since it is a short, squat, wide monster, it looms large in the ensuing debates. It was bought as a pot plant for our former house, to sleep on a poolside deck. There is argument as to who bought it. My elder daughter and I think it was bought from K-Mart by her then-boyfriend to ingratiate himself in 1973. My brother thinks he bought it for me as a present for my birthday the same year! It lasted on the pool deck 'til 1980 when we moved it to Lotus Island and planted it as a little tree in front of the cottage. There it grew like Topsy to a beautiful specimen, eventually twenty feet high but starting to interfere with the sea view. Moreover, Lotus Island is not South Carolina and the tree's summer blooms are sparse. Beautiful and fragrant, but sparse! Here, these are plants prized for their large glossy leaves.

I remember clearly one winter day remarking to the pianist that we had the best specimen of magnolia on Lotus Island. That night we had a heavy snowfall and the tree broke in half with the snow load. I was punished for my proud remark! Broad-leaved evergreens are a risk in snow load areas. There was serendipity, however, in this calamity, as the view returned, much to the pleasure of the pianist. Since then I have trimmed the magnolia, or had it trimmed, to maintain the view and it has become progressively more portly. The current controversy is that it is taking over the yard, produces few flowers, and requires arduous trimming to maintain its height. Moreover, it is now said to be a tree that is not a tree but rather a monster shrub. Despite this, I am adamant that it stays, since I have become even more attached to it, my guilt is assuaged, and I can claim to have the fattest magnolia on Lotus Island.

A So-called Lawn

Pojar and Mackinnon, in *Plants of Coastal British Columbia*, describe two hundred different grasses in coastal BC, Washington, and Alaska, most of which are indigenous to the area. Today I cut my so-called lawn, composed of a variety of these grasses, for the second time this year. When we moved here in August 1979, the pianist and I inherited a meadow, amongst other contributions of Mother Nature. The meadow grasses were three to five feet tall and mighty impressive. Over the years I have mowed our meadow regularly, turning it into what has become a passable lawn, though not of the same nature as its more civilized brethren from the seed store or turf farm.

The multiplicity of grass varieties in the so-called lawn remind me a little of the grade eight class at school. Some short, some tall, some plump, some skinny and pimply, but all quite beautiful and growing at different rates. Because of that characteristic, to give it a semblance of lawn it must be cut regularly or it looks dreadfully thatchy. Close mowing over time has led to a population shift to the finer-blade varieties. I have also, over time, planted store-bought seeds in some areas that I converted to lawn. These, of course, grow evenly and look well, even if one misses the occasional cut. In time, however, the sown lawn and the so-called lawn do begin to resemble one another, much like two people—such as the pianist and I—who have lived together for eons of time and are a product of the same living and ageing co-habits. I suppose if our lawns were in Lotus City I might feel a bit out of place, but here in the boondocks no one sees the lawn except those whom we choose to invite. I guess, in addition to putting your own stamp on a piece of ground, it's good to try to retain as much as possible of the gift that Mother Nature has freely given.

Dahlia Indigestion

I pulled all the dahlia tubers out from under the straw and tarps where they have been sleeping all winter. Even though it is warm enough on Lotus Island to winter them in the ground, our dirt is wet in the winter since we are below the Hundred Hills and with the excessive winter drainage they will rot. They have done so in the past when I was lazy one year and failed to lift them. Why we always learn the hard way I never know. They came through the winter with less than three percent rotted this year, which is pretty good for me. I used to wash and dust them before storage but now just shove them, dirt and all, under copious amounts of straw beneath tarps. The bulbs are particularly nice and plump this spring. Now I have to split them, as they are compounded and multiply compounded. Quite the job! I also have to haul and compost the straw.

I like dahlias better than most flowering plants since they are user-friendly, propagate like stink, and bloom all summer and fall. However, I suffer from dahlia indigestion since after the clumps are split I have too many tubers but am reluctant to discard the ones that might be destined to produce the winning bloom. I think you call this greed. The deer may browse the plants a little but they do trifling damage to them. The slugs are voracious with sprouting dahlias but a few early morning snips with the snippers will do it.

The sprouting bulbs may have an innate intelligence. Normally, it has been said, it's best to plant them when the oak leaves are the size of squirrels' ears. Oak leaf sizing is the litmus test for dahlia planting time? Not sure if this can be true. Is there weather wisdom in oak leaves? Is the positive squirrel-ear litmus test coincident with dahlia-bulb restlessness? This all seems like boondock wisdom. A Triumvirate of Nature communicating with one another? I can pick a young oak leaf and look at a tuber, but my squirrels won't stay still long enough to allow me to compare the sizing of the ears.

Houseplant Jungle

I once grew a Monstera deliciosa that became, over time, so big that the aerial roots grew into our green shag rug and broached the floorboards in our house in town. It leached out all the dye from the rug where it rooted. This was in the olden days when shag rugs were de rigueur. Needless to say, I was not popular with the pianist. The children and I had lugged this plant from the greenhouse to the living room annually for years on a toboggan after I repotted it into progressively larger and larger pots. Eventually it became so heavy we had to hammer two-by-fours into the pot for four people to carry it. I must have been mad. I eventually was forced to give it to the Crystal Gardens in Lotus City, then a civic arboretum. At least they sent a truck to pick it up, along with my obscenely large bird-of-paradise that had also been "over the top." My failing is I cannot easily get rid of plants that I have harboured for years but which have outgrown their space. I have not learned my lesson and now struggle with a thirty-year-old rubber tree (Fiscus elastica) on Lotus Island that is twenty feet tall and has started to become unruly and leaf-burned on top due to its proximity to a skylight. If I prune it, it leaks white rubber sap in great gushes and then develops a wild and crazy growth habit.

When we were in Israel years ago at the Church of the Beatitudes on the site of the Sermon on the Mount, north of the Sea of Galilee, there was a Fiscus elastica planted by Mussolini in 1934, the year I was born. He planted it in order to be blessed for his conquering of what was then Abyssinia. The tree was about eighty feet high by then, and was a beautiful tree despite the grotesque gesture of Mussolini planting on Jesus's stomping grounds. Imagine planting a tree in the spot where Jesus preached, "blessed be the peacemakers," to celebrate killing and conquering your neighbour. My house tree, however, is long, lank, and a victim of my own botanical hubris. It is not the plant's fault the growth habit is crazy! The pianist is into African violets and Streptocarpus. That makes more sense for little old people.

Heather and Heath

Walking on the Pentland Hills this spring with my son, a midlife eclectic gentleman, we observed the patches of Scottish heather on the hillsides, burned by rangers in a planned and programmed manner for renewal. Travelling a few years earlier in the fall with the pianist through Sutherland and Caithness, the hills were alive with purple heather and yellowing fern. The heather belongs! It seems indestructible. The heather is blooming today in my patch on Lotus Island. It is unruly, grey-green with dusty purple blooms, and greatly favoured by all manner of visiting little flying travelers, most of which I cannot identify. Entomology has been lost to me now.

I don't prune my heather and I can't burn my patch to renew it. Its cousin, the white heather, is also unruly and somewhat larger. It is so nice to have the muted colors of the fall bloom. Mixed in with the heathers is the heath. It, of course, is mostly spring-blooming, so it is presently at rest. Heath in most of the wet coast gardens is pruned rather tightly so the bloom is abundant and very showy. I don't think mine has ever had such a haircut. Some of the heath in the patch is fuzzy, tall shrub heath with small white bells in the spring. My patch, all told, looks like a population of adolescents. They seed themselves, so some new plants come along and new plants also take root from low branches, so they are a crowd, ranging in size and age and flowering! "Bless 'em all, bless 'em all, the young and the short and the tall!" Aside from water they need naught else! They are user-friendly! There is nothing vulgar about common *Calluna vulgaris*.

Rototill Your Compost Pile

After a hot, dry midsummer, the rain came for a few days and I rototilled my compost pile! It's a great way to mix the working material, but avoid the front-tine tiller. The rear-tine tiller gives much more control in mixing, and you are less likely to fall off the compost heap. The compost I have consists of shredded hedge cuttings with lots of leaf and old straw bales used earlier for dahlia bulb storage. These take time to digest. I throw some balanced fertilizer on it to speed up the working, and some of my nephew's Happy Farmer Bokashi with SCD Efficient Microbes! These latter two things are less important than the adequate mixing of the materials, and even more crucial still, the tiller brings up from below the thin year-old residual layer of compost I always leave behind when spreading the top material on the garden the previous fall. The layer of compost left behind is like the sourdough starter bread-makers prize and perpetuate for years. How could an old sourdough prospector manage to live and prospect without his cache of starter yeast to sustain him? Last year's retained compost layer is also like the residual tea leaves left in the cha-damari indentation in the Japanese tea ceremony's raku bowl. A ceremonial tea statement that "We never take all from the world!" We return the compost to the land from whence it came, but leave a little behind in the bottom of the pile as a starter for the next year's compost. This is practical as well as spiritual. We also leave a little compost remaining behind because we do not take all from the earth. Like the raku, which also is made from the earth, we leave a little tea in the raku bowl, like water in a rock pool. What is left behind is a spiritual reminder that we always owe a debt to life for renewal.

Learning from Bad Examples

Pity the poor student that in life had only superb teaching and exemplary teachers. I learned much from my own failures and from those whose failures surrounded me. Periodic teaching from bad examples provides one with the zeal and stimulus to do better and emulate the best teachers. The realization that one can do much better than that which has been offered will lead to renewed efforts on the part of the student. The stream of consciousness will be stimulated not only by good ideas but also, in the right hands, by ideas that are barren. There is not much in life that is absolute. Received wisdom has ebbed and flooded over time and often given way to new and further wisdom. We are hammered these days with polarized disputes on almost every subject imaginable.

We have been given five senses that allow us to come to our own conclusions. A sixth sense which can be awakened, intuition, is buried deep within everyone. The seventh sense is crucial to all of us: common sense! Gardeners will observe the world around them on their own terms. Smell the roses and all else! Touch and feel the rough and the smooth. Listen to the sounds of the natural world. Taste the abundance that has been freely given. Wait and listen for the spirit to awaken one to fresh beginnings. Ask oneself, "Does this make ordinary sense?" Know that all experiences are teaching tools, good and bad. Accept those tools with curiosity, enthusiasm, and grace. That's what molds the collagen in character!

Ambivalence

Mrs. M was a pioneer member of the garden maternity of Lotus Island in the eighties when I was developing my garden. She was an experienced market gardener, gave advice freely, and suggested to me that asparagus would grow well on our plot, situated where it was. I undertook to plant a substantial asparagus garden under her direction but was reluctant to fence it in as this would interfere with our view of the harbour. An asparagus plot of size is no small undertaking since it requires two to three years of development, significant fertilization, persistent weeding by hand, and care to avoid damage to the roots and incipient spears. It's also inadvisable to cut the developing spears during the formative period. I applied a top dressing of seaweed to the plot in large measure since she advised that and suggested the salinity would be advantageous.

To my irritation, a doe came visiting my patch of asparagus at frequent intervals, munching on my spears in prolonged browsing, as deer are often wont to do when they find something good. She wouldn't take shooing seriously and came back, so one day I lost control, became enraged, and chucked a stone at her. Unfortunately, the stone hit her in the adductor region of the right thigh and she fell to the ground, lying on her side, thrashing wildly in pain and fear. I was filled with dread and felt like a monster, believing that I had permanently damaged this creature who was simply behaving normally. It flashed through my head that I had no means to arrest her pain. After a few minutes of writhing around she got up and walked away without a discernable limp. I breathed a sigh of thankfulness. I was under no illusion that she had learned a lesson and would not return. I, however, had learned a lesson, and that was that she was doing what any deer would do without meaning any harm to me. I had not reciprocated in kind. I meant harm. Failing to look at one's ambivalence is a mistake. Judgement will be intelligent if one does examine ambivalence. The old saw of watching your enemy drive over the cliff with your new car can be avoided by doing the right thing. Make a friend of the enemy, buy an old car, fence the asparagus patch in the spring and summer with temporary fencing, and enjoy unimpeded viewing of the harbour and the deer in the late summer and beyond.

Hedge trimmer

As an elderly eclectic gentleman I am too feeble to manage trimming a large hedge and controlling a heavy long-handled gas hedge trimmer without some creative inventiveness! My Rube Goldberg apparatus was a simple structure that employed a crutch secured to a boat engine mount, both readily available in every household of decrepits living by the beach. When I tried my invention it was somewhat awkward and only moderately effective. The hedge I have inherited was planted by Mother Nature and consists of—among other things—hurtful, thorny Rosa vulgaris, blackberry vines, and hawthorns. The object of my invention allowed the gas-driven hedge cutter to perch on the handhold of the crutch, which took the weight of the seven-foot trimmer. It protected me from the thorny hedge. The engine mount base could be moved every four feet along the hedge and the hedge trimmed in a horizontal arc-like fashion. The hedge height achieved would be determined by the height of the crutch handhold from the ground, which got rid of the need for string or eyeball. I thought it was a good idea, but my son-in-law came along, tried it briefly, and then just cut the hedge without my Rube Goldberg creation, since he is an energetic eclectic gentleman. Since my hedge is six or seven feet deep, trimmed to four feet high at the lawn, twelve feet at the water side, and is two hundred feet long, it is a daunting task! I was blessed with his help. I did the mop-up work and shredded the clippings the following day. Thank goodness for my son-in-law. If my family and friends abandon me, I may have to revert to my invention. I want to avoid being a laughingstock. It's getting harder!

Community Vegetable Garden

Lotus City provided parcels of vacant land for people who wished to grow their own vegetables and didn't have access to appropriate land. The parcels were individual plots, each twenty by fifty feet, adjacent to one another. There was piped-in water and an atmosphere of camaraderie and competition throughout the growing year. The plots became highly individualistic and reflected the personalities of those that toiled in the soil. The plot the pianist and I had one year was in a community garden surrounded by a newly developed subdivision of houses. In an effort to improve my plot I answered an ad for manure. The man who answered said he could provide good pig manure. I asked him if it was mature and well-composted and he assured me that it was, so I ordered a full truckload. When he backed up to my plot and raised the truck box, the product began to slide out, and I mean slide! It was immediately apparent that "dump" truck was the apt description of the vehicle and its content. The pig manure was of recent origin. Shortly after the dump, I could see the windows of my proximate neighbours open and then quickly close. The smell was evil! I raced home and engaged my son to bring his gumboots and help me spread and till in the manure before we were cited for olfactory offense. We did a good job. I confess the cauliflower and broccoli that year were of winning quality.

The Fraser River Delta

When one leaves the islands of the Salish Sea and drives through the Fraser River delta to Olympic City in October, the fields off the highway in the river delta are spectacularly red. These are cranberry and blueberry fields turning to their fall colors. One sees very little on the highway, eye on the ferry traffic ahead, but take a few minutes, leave the highway, and wander a back road or two and you are in for an enormous treat. There is nothing more attractive than miles of orange, red, and brown for the short magical period Mother Nature and the berry farmer provide. Both berries grow best in the peaty, boggy delta soil supplied over the centuries by the flooding of the Fraser River and the rotting vegetation. The sight of the fields is thrilling and at the same time sobering, knowing that the Fraser undergoes a major flood every fifty years. I remember feeling the same thrill with the colourful magnificence of miles of heather and fern massed in the hills of Caithness and Perthshire. The capacity of Mother Nature to provide the vegetation that will thrive in these difficult particular soil types, allowing a thriving duo-culture, whether planned by man or Mother Nature, is an interesting departure from the multiple mixed vegetation we usually see in BC. Seems there are plants for every location! Darwin would be interested by the evolution of species and their adaptation. So would Mendel. So should we!

The Four Elements

I was watering and turning my compost the other day and thinking of Empedocles. He, according to Will Durant, lived 500 to 430 BC. You may know that he was the first to describe the four elements—fire, water, earth, and air—of which the world is composed. This understanding was foundational to the classical philosophers that followed. It's still true, and my compost tells me that is so. As I attended my compost, which was mostly straw and green vegetable matter, I added water and the pile in time became very hot. Deep down it was breaking up and becoming soil: warm, richly brown, and particulate. I piled it loosely as it needs to breathe in order to work. It is true that the four elements are extraordinarily complex and diverse in their highly developed state, but compost is the great leveller.

All complexities are reduced to earth by means of air, heat, and water. Even you and I, in all our complexity, will be returned to dust, and if we are burned in the undertaker's compost bin, the heat will be much faster and hotter than my compost. So the compost pile, through air and water and heat, becomes earth, as does all else. Ironically, Empedocles died after the fashion of his philosophy. He became convinced that he was a god and could fly, so hurled himself into the mouth of a volcano. He couldn't fly and so hurtled through the air and heat of the volcano and, carrying his own moisture, undoubtedly returned to dust.

Birdbrain

This apparently disparaging comment about forgetful or thoughtless requires reexamination! For the past two months in the late fall the robins at our plot on Lotus Island were notable for their complete absence. They were abundant during the early fall. Nothing had changed that would have occasioned their departure. The worms and bugs remained in plentiful numbers. One thing, however, is noted, and that is that the holly berries were not quite ripe during that period. The robins, of course, are omnivorous. They don't exist on protein alone. They must have, if not an internal clock, an internal calendar, or alternatively a readily available Day Runner. The holly berries are now ripened! The robins are not "birdbrains"; they appeared in spades about four days ago. They started in the orchard by turning up the leaves in the windrows I made with the blower that Eddy, my handyman, and I haven't been able to drag to the compost yet. Tossing their heads they threw leaves helter-skelter, seeking the cringing bug or worm. Once I saw them I knew what they were really after. The appetizer may have been bugs and worms, but the entree consisted of my holly berries. The assault on the holly tree can start about the fifth of December and despite it being a loaded fifty-foot tree they clean it up in ten to fifteen days! This year the tree was a bit late in ripening like everything else. How they knew? That kind of timing doesn't suggest a birdbrain is forgetful or thoughtless. They may not be able to spell well, but they are not stupid. Neither am I because I cut all the holly we needed three days ago, preempting their action. They can go to it all they want now! The only drawback to this feeding frenzy is the wider-distributed seedlings I have to weed next year from the droppings.

The Motley Crew

As I march through the commercial nursery greenhouses from time to time I feel a touch of envy over the pristine row on row of abundantly flowering and verdant houseplants for sale. They smack of the beauty of the young, but are often bought, treasured, and turfed when they are no longer so beautiful. If you see perennials as furnishing to stage your house for beauty, you will see no sense in any alternative value to them. However, if you anthropomorphize your houseplants, you will, as we have over many years, create a confederation of a motley crew. The pianist has said from time to time that we should get rid of some of these plants since they are too big, some are ugly, and they are taking over the house and greenhouse. I don't disagree with her observations about ugly and large, but have so far avoided implementing some of these suggestions. A good marriage seeks compromise. I also have a bottom line and have euthanized and buried the worst of them in the compost. Such an act is love in action since they will rise again in new form when the compost is planted. The survivors are old friends. They can be primped up to be at least acceptable, but it does become more and more of a struggle. They provide memories of the olden days when they were young and beautiful. I am not a callow person. I am loyal. The old plants can rely on us to give geriatric care, to water regularly, to avoid rich food, to amputate at times to stave off death. We are still more a happy home for the elderly than a hospice. We share their joy.

The Pansy

The pansy, or for that matter the shrinking violet: what misnomers for timid or shy people! They are tough little plants! The pansies are anything but "pansies" and the violets may be modest in size but they are mighty! We had minus-six centigrade here on Lotus Island last week. The foundation box chrysanthemums turned black but the pansies didn't turn a hair. How could anyone have taken these plants as a metaphor for timidity? The pansy was always the favourite flower of the pianist. As a little girl she saw the flower as a face. I can see that! Anthropomorphizing again! Particularly, for me as well, the yellow and brown petal arrangement is about as close to a little face as any flower I can think of. They not only are tough, they are modest, but they are not in your face. Never mistake modesty, shyness, or timidity for weakness, in man or plant! I am long enough in the tooth to know that with other people or plants, what you see is not always what you get! On the island, the pansy winters over beautifully, waiting for that first soft warm breath in February to flourish when underplanted with the daffodils in the foundation boxes. The reflected heat from the house allows them to spring forward. Being greeted by these harbingers of spring as we leave the house puts a spring in our steps as well as in our hearts.

Deer Damage Coping

On Lotus Island the deer have free "reign." They are medium-sized mule deer and are no more skittish than cows in a pasture. There are virtually no predators (other than cars), with the exception of a few hunters in the fall; there are no trophy bucks here. The odd hunter claims to be after meat. Whatever! One of the reasons the deer are bold is that dogs do not run free on Lotus Island. There are many sheep farmers and they will shoot any dog that harasses their sheep. Dog lovers contain their animals. The garden damage the deer do is confined to a few plant species, so most of us have avoided planting the vulnerable. In my garden, of course, I have not followed my own advice. At risk are Japanese laurel (Aucuba japonica), camellia, a cedar variety (Smaragd), azalea, and small-leaf rhododendrons. Also vulnerable are most spring bulbs other than daffodils. Deer also eat bergenia and some sedum. Deer occasionally chew dahlia. Since they browse and are alert, they seldom stay more than a few minutes in any one place. Their pattern of trail-walking is absolutely consistent and predictable in time and space. I use smelly deer repellent, Plantskydd, on the deer-vulnerable plants. If I spray on sunnier days it lasts one or two months. Once they've tasted a sprayed leaf, they change their pattern of browsing. The presence of the deer on our lot, within proximity, is a delight we can only enjoy if they aren't fenced out. Aside from rhubarb and globe artichokes, vegetables either need a fence or, better still, plan to buy your vegetables from an organic marketer! Anyway, it's not the end of the world to do so. I always think a home vegetable gardener spends a hundred dollars of effort and seed to grow ten dollars worth of produce. I admit I justify my own idiosyncrasies to obtain whatever compromise I arrive at! We used to say about a particular surgeon, "Frequently wrong but never in doubt!" If I stick my neck out about the garden I guess I might also qualify for that characterization. Still, the other axiom to follow in medicine was, "First, do no harm." That's the one I choose.

Snow load

The bane of a gardener's life can be a wet snow load followed by a sharp frost. The evergreens here on the wet coast, rhododendrons, evergreen magnolia, sweet bay, and tree heath undergo breakage if the snow load is on brittle branches. Trying to brush the snow off in the cold snap adds to the breakage. Best is to pray! Over the last several years I have had two mature prune plum trees completely topple over due to wind and heavy snow load and inadequate pruning on my part. Prune plums are shallow-rooted trees and the above-ground growth has to match the underground growth. I didn't follow that rule. Gardening 101! I have a Victoria plum that has an off-balance growth habit and I think it will be next to bite the dust. That plum is not plumb! The deciduous trees are by and large protected against snow load by their nature. There is nothing so revealing in the winter as the lovely tracery that the deciduous trees create against the sky. When they are in full leaf they do not reveal their true shape or the unique characteristics and variety of the species. Having a garden or wilderness tramp on a nice day when the snow is off the branches is a visual treat, observing the tree shapes in their skeletal nakedness. If you look down as well as up, you can also read the diary in the snow left by all your little visitors: a tracery of who they were and where they went.

Prepared for Snow

Lotus Island, on the Salish Sea, often gets two weeks of snow around Christmas time. This is a hilly island and it's tough to get around. Because we are part of the wet coast, the precipitation is sometimes huge. The pianist and I are ready! We are accumulating a reserve of foodstuffs to sustain us and our guests through a period of sequestration. We have purchased a scoop shovel. Our four-wheel-drive SUV has new snow tires. Wood is cut and kindling is ready for our airtight and our fireplace. Four bags of road salt have been purchased and stored. Candles and flashlights and a wind-up radio are at hand. A small generator is in the basement with gas available. The liquor cabinet has been fortified. I have wrapped all the outside taps in burlap and the garden standpipes have been drained. The lining in our jackets has been inserted. That's the benefit of being an old fart: you have time on your hands and obsession on your mind. Having done all this, of course, is a guarantee that it won't snow. If you don't want something to happen, prepare! If you want the telephone to ring with an important subject, don't hover around the phone; sit on the toilet and the phone will always ring. I am unlikely to receive much in the way of thanks from the denizens of Lotus Island for preventing the snow from coming, since they don't resort to magical thinking. After all, they probably don't believe that King Canute could hold back the tides with his hand either!

Whitewash Cover-up

The pianist and I live on a moraine soil that has a plethora of rocks of all sizes. In over thirty-two years of tillage, digging and raking a large part of this acre, many of these treasures have been uncovered. I never found a rock I didn't like. They are almost always round, since they were ground up and rolled down the mountain in days of yore to create the moraine. I raided the rocks from Mother Nature where she had placed them and used them "au naturel" to bank flowerbeds, slopes for inter-planting, and to outline my homely little garden features.

I suppose in earlier times it was thought that naked rocks, like everyone else, should be clothed. When I was a boy it was de rigueur on the prairies to whitewash your rocks. Every civic center, all the railway terminals, RCMP stations, centenary parks, and many businesses had whitewashed rocks. Rocks were supposed, then, to be ugly in their natural state so were clothed by liming! This was a job I did at the railroad stations we lived in. Whitewash became part of the lexicon for cover-up of things you wanted to hide, even sepulchres. It could be considered an old expression of "lipstick on the pig." As if rocks and pigs were dirty! Whitewashing structures as well as sins must have extended well beyond our little prairie towns. Tom Sawyer was whitewashing Aunt Polly's fence even before my days of yore. I cannot get over how unnatural that convention of whitewashed rock gardens seems. What's more, one had to whitewash repeatedly, or the truth eventually became exposed.

Eagle Attack

A while back we were watching a bevy of bufflehead ducks in the harbour with an eagle cruising above them. These are diving ducks. Suddenly the eagle spiralled down and the ducks scattered. The eagle seemed initially to have missed the strike but a lone duck remained and stayed on the surface. The eagle made a lazy circle over the area and then dropped in a long sloping descent to the lone duck. The duck dived at just the right moment and the eagle seemed to have missed. This scenario was repeated at least five times and each time the duck dived for a shorter period. The eagle was relentless. It appeared to rake the duck on its last foray and then returned to pick up the duck, which, it seemed, could no longer dive. The eagle flew off with its prey in its talons. I felt a sense of horror for the duck. Even though I know this is part of life, I am always struck with the brutality of reality. Predators have to eat and supply their families. Eagles are large birds with big appetites and they eat a variety of land and marine life, including ducks. Still, I find it discomforting. I can't be a hypocrite, however, since I too am part of the food chain and I am omnivorous. My meat-eating is at arm's length from the killing fields. Like many others, my action is sanitized. I see it as acceptable since I thrive on denial. I am comforted by the fact that cognitive dissonance is part of the human condition—except possibly for those who never feel confused.

Shred and Burn

Living as we do in a bucolic rural area, burning or shredding the cellulose we accumulate is optional. The noise of my Bearcat shredder doesn't bother anyone and the smoke raised by the burning of larger wooden limbs and trash wood is not offensive to my distant neighbours. I usually burn on the beach. I like the shredded material because it returns fibre to the soil when composted and supplies useful material for chipped pathways, an advantage on the wet coast. In the wet months I can burn all the paper trash in the incinerator as well and use the ash in the compost for phosphorous. All told this is a pretty good system if you live in the country.

I love power tools for gardening. I couldn't shred or use a blower or my weed eater or power washer in Lotus City without constantly irritating my neighbours, who were mostly urban green. In my medical practice I saw too many chainsaw injuries to be comfortable with one. I have avoided that useful tool with a bit of reluctance. Four-fifths of a loaf is better than no loaf. I hand-turn my compost heap but also use a five-horsepower Honda tiller to mix it when it starts to return to black. Having the capacity to turn most of the biodegradable material back into the ground gives me a feeling of providing a redeeming activity. I, at least, am recycling most of my own trash and not relying on others. That gives me some satisfaction! Self-righteousness, however, is not redeeming. Sorry!

Sex in the Island

It's spring on Lotus Island and the harbour is abuzz with incipient lovemaking activity! The oystercatchers have returned. The couples are never far apart from one another. They always announce their return with high piping whistling. The blue herons are battling over tree space for nesting in the large Douglas fir over our studio. My daughter and her friend counted six herons squabbling, apparently about which branch should be allotted to them. The pianist thinks some of them are yearlings longing to return to their old nests and being kicked out. I'm not sure how many herons constitute a heronry and who is in control. The diving ducks, buffleheads and mergansers, are still awaiting the herring return so they can fatten up and migrate elsewhere for nesting. The dabbling ducks (American widgeons) will eat the eelgrass with even more benefit once the herring eggs are on it and the gulls and crows will feed on the loose eggs lapping at the shoreline. All that protein enhances fertility! In the meantime the herring are on the way. The harbour seals are about to take pleasure in one another and later dine on herring. If you have a dog on your walk on the beach, the seals follow you with great interest. The small birds in the hedgerow at the beach are busy nest-building in the hedge. The little males stand a vigilant guard on top of the spent black bamboo stakes that I leave for them. The pianist is an eagle devotee and tells me they are now in the process of nest renewal and refurbishing and will soon continue their connubial relationship. There are a lot more interesting varieties of sex on Lotus Island (and less inhibition and neurosis) than on *Sex in the City*.

Gladiolus and Mums

Thirty or forty years ago the gladiolus was a stunning exhibition flower that engaged the best of growers in producing, propagating, and hybridizing a truly noble species! The demise of the exhibition gladiolus and its retreat to third-rate florist varieties has been caused and accompanied by the demise of the home vegetable and cut flower garden. The gladiolus was never a suitable plant for a landscaping scene and landscaping is now all the rage. Landscaping sells because zeitgeist rules! It's the end of an era but it's too bad. Sure, the fall fairs always have exceptions but the gladioli exhibited are remarkably few. In the days of yore my dad could buy large corms of old varieties like Red Charm (for $4.00 a hundred) and Elizabeth the Queen (for $5.00 a hundred) from Milton Jack at Hatzic Lake. With that volume available you could produce champion specimens. The range of named varieties available was huge. Now the only class bulb farm I know of is Summerville's in New Jersey and the prices are prohibitive. It's the same decline in numbers with the chrysanthemum aficionados.

The mum group in Lotus City is a small and talented bunch. They grow the most beautiful muted disbuds you've ever seen but their ranks thin every year despite the extraordinary attempts they make to recruit new enthusiasts. Again popularity falls short, due to the need for a cut flower garden for champion mums, rather than everything dedicated to landscape. It is sad to see skills sacrificed on the altar of landscape cosmetics. Surely there is room for both styles of garden. If more people were encouraged to grow these flowers again, the cost would be affordable, the beauty pageants would flower, and the standards would be maintained.

Impetuous Gardening

A man without a plan is like Don Quixote mounting his horse and riding off in all directions. A man with a bad plan is even less well-off! I had a wet spot in my garden that was marshy in the winter and so, some time ago, I thought I would plant cranberries there since they grow well here in the Pacific Northwest. The peaty bogs in the Fraser delta grow beautiful blueberries and cranberries and the fields are spectacular in the fall when they turn deep reddish-orange. I phoned a commercial cranberry farmer in the delta to ask what to do to plant a cranberry bog. He said they mowed the plants after harvest and I was welcome to cuttings since they threw them away. There is nothing better than free. I drove to the delta farm and he gave me two full garbage bags of his mowings. I built a bed with a substantial soil addition in my wet area and spent a long time planting my cuttings in a bed five feet by thirty feet. The cuttings were about four to six inches high. Most of them took, but so did the weeds. It was frightful. My little transplants were inundated with weeds. The task of weeding was daunting and after a half day of labour and scant inroads I realized I was defeated. Too impetuous—bad planning! I should have summer-fallowed for one or two seasons before starting such a project. Too big a hand in the cookie jar! Eyes too big for the stomach! Besides, I rationalized, "How many cranberries do you really need?" It was really just the idea. Another fruit to grow! Another idea to try! I transplanted my Gunnera into the erstwhile cranberry bed. Gunnera is much more user-friendly.

The Golden Apple; Quince

"I would fly to the coast of apples of which many tales are told, the far Hesperian shore where the mighty Lord of ocean forbids all further voyaging and marks the sacred limits of heaven, which Atlas holds. There the immortal streams flow fresh by the couch of God where he lies with his lovely ones—and earth, the mother of life, yields up blessings of harvest to enrich a bliss that never ends."*

Sounds like Lotus Island, doesn't it? Quince—the fruiting tree, not the flowering shrub—is of Mediterranean origin. It grew best there, but worked its way northward over the centuries and also grows on the islands in the Salish Sea. Here, it ripens in November and is golden. Undoubtedly the "apple" the Greeks and those of the Levant referred to was the quince, since apples as we know them would find that climate unacceptable. The pianist's and my greeting and thank-you card, courtesy of Euripides, is a reflection of the fact that here both the apple and quince and, for that matter, the medlar, all flourish on this small collection of islands in the Salish Sea, which are said to have a Mediterranean climate. I surmise the Hesperides were the mythical guardians of the golden apple, the quince. I am, too, though I am not mythical. Can you blame me for liking it here?

*Euripides, 484–406 BC (from Hippolytus)

Unnatural Act

I was removing, with difficulty, a string of outside Christmas lights from the quince tree. Some of the smaller branches were traumatized as the electrical wires clung to them and the freezing cold had rendered the branches rather brittle. As I was working away on the stepladder a small voice said, "You've made me look like a tart!" Then the voice said, "You've spent a long time yapping about Mother Nature and how organic you are, and you even quoted a poem about me, and now you have made me into a freak!" I must say I was taken aback by this tree's assertion, as I hadn't meant any disrespect. I didn't think it was unseemly to string lights on living bones but now I realize it is an unnatural act and has nothing to do with Christmas either!

"I guess you are right that I am a hypocrite," I said, "but it was out of ignorance rather than intent."

"No way," the quince said, "You have made such heavy weather of your connection to the vegetable world and apparently worshipped the dialogue between us. It gives us the suspicion now that you are a person who talks a good game but has little real understanding or respect for living bones. Rather than your feeble attempt to illuminate me, try to illuminate yourself!"

Well, you can readily see that I felt pretty crushed, particularly since she has provided faithfully every year beautiful quince for jellies and preserves, a home every year for the western flycatchers that grace our life, and never develops powdery mildew. Our quince is sweet! They have obviously discussed the matter in the orchard and I am properly reprimanded. I have assured her that I will not repeat any unnatural acts in the future and will scale down my rhetoric, beating my breast about how connected I am, when they really know better!

Peripheral Vision

When Hercule Poirot solves a difficult case it is because he sees more than meets the eye. When the radiologist focuses on the center of the radiograph, looking at the condition for which the image was taken and neglecting to look at the edges of the film for other things, stuff gets overlooked. The great painters spend as much time on the periphery of the painting as the golden mean. There is a lesson here for gardeners who would be true to their craft. It is not just what is seen that is important, but that which is not clearly seen. That which must be looked for! Within the boundaries of our plot, applied with brushstrokes over the years, there are intimate details and secrets that only we know about. You probably value the unseen, the secret, and the inobvious as much as the familiar. If we neglect these elements within our boundaries, we will not have a private place we can choose to share (or not share) with someone who loves a garden as much as we do. Intimacy means sharing secrets as well as triumphs or disasters. They come in ample supply in the garden for all of us. Humility is a chastening thing, but it leads to knowledge. I never learned much from my successes, but plenty from my failures. As Hannah, who quoted Leonard Cohen, says, "There is a crack in everything. That's how the light gets in." Give yourself a still, small place in the garden that is not for display, but only for those that can see more than meets the eye.

Sex in the Greenhouse

Every day I water my greenhouse tomatoes, then tie them up as they race upward along with the cukes. I fertilize my tomato blossoms at the same time. I have no birds or bees in the greenhouse so the tomatoes have to manage with my brush. The cukes are parthenogenetic so can exist without the brush of an elderly eclectic gentleman. The tomatoes need cross-fertilizing, but are of the same variety, so they have a lot in common and will give rise to a homogenous crowd of fruit without the potential for new and interesting offspring from different varieties. The little blossoms have responded to my dusting with enormous production. There is every reason why tomatoes were originally termed the "love apple" (pomme d'amour). They respond with gusto! They are fruitful! They were feared to cause uncontrolled eroticism. They fit the bill, "go forth and multiply."

I go down the row and then up the row, moving the pollen dust to the right and left in order to give the best exposure. Just remember these tomato blossoms are captive creatures. I worry about what they think of me. Do they see me as just a pimp, transferring pollen from the unwanted to the indifferent? Or as a member of a ménage a trois, sticking my nose into a group where I do not belong? It makes me sheepish! They have an inability to live and thrive autonomously because I have confined them to a pot and limited their horizons. The blossoms have no control of their own lives and scope because of the cloistered situation I have placed them in. Since I have not given them the freedom to seek fertilization by natural means, I owe it to them to protect and nurture. I know for them I am second-best and I always thank them. Mother Nature also loves them both; parthenogenetic or pomme d'amour, she says, walk with pride. I don't know about the cukes' origin but tomatoes, potatoes, tobacco, and siphlis were exported to the world from the Americas. A mixed blessing, but a conquering assembly.

Birdie Num Nums

In the ongoing battle to defend one's berry patch against the avian horde, care has to be exercised so that one doesn't fatally trap the birdie in one's net. If one is going to grow birdie num nums, prepare to succeed occasionally and fail often. I have given up netting the loganberries on the fence, but they are so prolific the birds always leave enough for us. Strawberries are easier to net and the birds don't get caught. We just lay the nets on the top of the plants. Now that the strawberries are finished, I have mowed the patch to encourage new growth. Raspberries are impossible for me to effectively net. Birds always seem to get in, but the few robins do little damage since the berries come on so fast. I am ambivalent about berry-eating birds since we have such a multitude behaving normally; I guess it's just about food competition, them and us. I planted the berries but cannot claim ownership! I can't blame the birds, as their tune is harmonized to Mother Nature's song, not mine. We have two sweet cherry trees and we never get a cherry! The birds eat them before they turn pink. Oh well! I have spent the last three days patching holes in the blueberry nets. I'm winning! For the pianist and me, blueberries are people num nums. We draw the line at birds and blueberries. The birds can be voracious for blueberries and it seems mainly the young, speckled-breasted robins that think, since they were born here, this is their place; they are incautious and brazen. The impelling reason to patch all the holes in the nets is because the young birds can find their way in but not out. I make morning rounds to shoo them out if they are imprisoned. They can get inextricably tangled in the netting and I don't want a funereal blueberry patch with dead young robins dangling on the netting. It is inharmonious to pick blueberries in the midst of a grotesquerie!

Blueberry Nets

We have had large small-mesh old fishing nets (probably herring or anchovy) for many years. The nets are still serviceable though they need repairs from time to time. They are much better than the more rigid plastic garden netting. My granddaughter, my son-in-law, and I put up the nets on our blueberry patch last week. It's a big patch, twenty by fifty-five feet, and takes a lot of net. The robins are relentless in their attempts to breach our defenses. Tying the several nets together and propping the ceiling net with long struts is a major undertaking for the day. If you don't net your blueberries here on this island in the Salish Sea, you will not have any blueberries. They ripen, of course, in sequence over a three-month period within the clusters rather than all at once. That is why commercial berries are expensive; they require being selectively hand-picked. Labour-intensive! The smart birds would selectively pick, or peck, the ripe ones on a daily basis if they have a chance and a flock could keep up with the ripe berries if they were not netted. The first year that I had a big crop in the eighties I didn't net and wondered why my berries never ripened 'til the season was half over. We remove the nets in the early fall since the foliage colour is spectacular.

The blueberries are user-friendly as they do not need spraying and produce from both old and new wood, so pruning is simply tidying. We're looking forward to three months' bounty! The pianist is known amongst our family and friends for blueberry pancakes and blueberry muffins. The pièce de résistance, however, is blueberry pie, built with fifty percent cooked and fifty percent raw berries, poured into a baked pie crust, topped with whipped cream.

Doomed

The northwestern crow is normally a gregarious animal. A broken-winged crow walked up the path in front of my window a few days ago. That waddling, bowlegged strut was altered by the broken right wing that dragged on the stones. As I watched, his walk was slow and deliberate. He knew, I think, that he was doomed. He had a stoic look on his face that said it all. I don't understand the entire multiple, complex phrasing the crow uses, but as an orthopedic surgeon I know body language, gait abnormality, and skeletal injury pretty well, and I know from that body language the crow knew he was walking to the abyss. He was silent, but though there was nothing to hear, I was listening. I never thought I would see him again and put it out of my mind. I was working in the orchard two days later and there he was, still alive, still hopping from bush to bush, hiding to avoid detection—hiding from predators, both his own kind and the raptors! Still doomed. It doesn't seem fair. You or I may break a leg or arm and it is often a minor inconvenience, rarely if ever a tragedy, and hardly are we doomed. If we were, we would not likely bear our fate with the stoic silence and grim recognition of the injured crow. He gave no quarter and received none.

Canada Geese and Black Aphids

Today I observed two events of interest as I toiled in the soil. The egg shakers from Fish and Wildlife clearly missed two nests of Canada geese and as a result of this oversight, two sets of parents have finally ventured out into the harbour at Lotus Island with four adolescents each. The adolescents are about half-size and are all brown with a slight white backside. They stick closely together with one another and their parents because the eagles are actively feeding their fledglings. About another fifty adult geese, bereft of goslings, hunker along, trailing after the families. The trailers are victims of the egg shakers, no doubt. I guess we need to control the Canada geese population, but the forlorn trailers seem sad. Don't ask me how I know, I just do! For some reason the geese never come up to the lawn these days but stick to the harbour and the seaweed food source, particularly eelgrass. That saves a lot of shoe-fouling goose poop. They are enormously sedate and hardly honk unless they fly.

The other event to report is the heat has really struck here on Lotus Island and that means, with rapid dahlia growth and humidity, the black aphids have appeared on the early flower bud stems. There are a few, but not enough ladybugs around to eat them; despite this help, the aphid colonies grow rapidly. Black aphids are remarkably easy to deal with mechanically by daily inspection, wiping them clean off the stem with finger and thumb, and then top-spraying with water. The pianist thinks I should try Avon Bubble Bath so I am going to give it a go. A little soap never hurt plant or beast. The aphids seem endemic rather than epidemic, so a daily round and a little early attention is what is required for the dahlias that are afflicted. No poisons are necessary! No other crisis is looming large on Lotus Island today. Good news is not banal! Amor de Cosmos would have fitted in perfectly here.

Raspberry and Pea pickin'

My dad would never let the children pick raspberries or peas, "bless his pea-pickin' heart." He was afraid they would tramp on next year's raspberry canes, and they did! He knew they would pick an unripe raspberry with one hand and inadvertently tear off the whole cluster, ripe and unripe, and they did. He also complained that they didn't have soft hands so they squashed the ripe berries. I heard this all my childhood so I have followed his advice. He was right! "The same applies to peas," he groused, "They pull them straight off with one hand and that rips the vine from the ground. They have to use two hands, one to hold the stem and one to pick the pod. I don't want dried peas on the rootless vine after they leave!" When I was a boy we didn't, as I recall, have the pea varieties that ripen all at once like the commercial growers want. They pick them once and that's it. Our old-fashioned peas: Lincoln, Tall Telephone, and others, produced over time, so preserving the vines was crucial. He was right, "bless his cotton pickin', pea picker heart," even if he was singing a note from Tennessee Ernie Ford. I was picking raspberries today for the first time and thinking back to all of this. My raspberry patch has about five varieties planted randomly over the years as fill-ins. They vary in size and colour, mellowness and tartness, and date of ripening. Colour is OK as an indicator, but for me, because of ripe colour differences, ascertaining texture from a gentle squeeze with such variable berries is more accurate. My gentle squeeze is softer than a good retriever's mouth. I'm careful of my new canes and always pick with two hands. I've given up on the peas since the California quail find the sprouting plants delicious and the feral bunnies that have arrived would certainly feel the same if they had the chance.

Mouse

Every house, including ours, has night sounds. It's been particularly cold on Lotus Island this week and the temperature gradients between the inside and the outside make the beams and studs shift and squeak and crack a little, the wind shakes the house an infinitesimal degree, to which it nevertheless objects, and the boughs of the cedar brush it gently. The sleeper who is hypervigilant also hears his ear and head contact on the pillow, his tinnitus, the bruit of the carotid pulse at times, and the crow on the roof. These sounds we have become accustomed to; they are unique to our house. Another's house sounds have different singularity. At four o'clock this morning I awoke to a new and unaccustomed sound. Was it the icemaker dropping chunked ice, an intruder, or something else? As I went down the stairs into the kitchen where the sound was coming from, it seemed to be a metallic sound originating from the tile floor. There had been a suggestion that an uninvited visitor had arrived the day before and I had set a mousetrap that night on the floor beside a baseboard with bait of peanut butter. In the trap was a mouse and it was alive and struggling. The metallic sound came from the thrashing around on the tile. The mouse probably ventured further into the trap than usual to gnaw at the bait so his head was not crushed and he was caught in the trap by the body. I have always had a primal fear of vermin, a legacy from my mother and the Middle Ages. I could deal, albeit with difficulty, with a dead mouse, but a living, wiggling, squiggling, leg-and-tail-waving mouse in agony is a different matter.

I went back to bed to await its death and silence. I couldn't sleep, however, assailed with thoughts of the waning life force with the reminder from the continuing sounds emanating from the kitchen floor. I took my courage and went back and put the mouse outside on the deck. Silence! This morning at eight o'clock he was dead and had struggled a further eighteen inches, dragging the trap from where I laid him on the deck. I'm sorry! I must kill! Rest in peace.

The California Quail

This Edenic patch called Lotus Island is within the most northern range for the California quail, a species which we have in abundance! They are without doubt the most picturesque addition to any garden. Here they seem to have several sets of chicks throughout the season; the chicks resemble little walnuts scurrying around, always close to cover near the underbrush. Several adults can be seen guarding a family of up to a baker's dozen little walnuts, parents and aunties all clicking vociferously if danger lurks or cover is needed. Lots of thick cover will assure you of a cavalcade of these feathered friends in your garden. I guess I really don't care if they eat all my new pea shoots. The quail have very little protection from the predators, crows and raptors. We have many eagles, hawks, crows, and ravens. I hate to see the carnage but I suppose it's the way of the world. On the one hand, most creatures, including us, are engaged in eating one another. On the other hand—on the bright side—Al Capp invented the Shmoo, which love to be eaten. I keep kidding myself. In my opinion the quail is the closest thing I know that physically resembles the Shmoo. Given the hypervigilance of the adult quail and the obedience of the offspring to the clicks, it's unlikely that the California quail is enchanted with the prospect of being eaten. The quail, along with the bunny, has the survival capacity as a species to endure by way of procreative ability. Lucky for us!

The Grinches and the Olympic Flame

It's Halloween on Lotus Island and the Olympic flame is arriving here at 2:30 p.m. by seaplane. It will be here for half an hour or so and many young people and families will be able to see it and be thrilled by it. However, we have a large number of homegrown Grinches on Lotus Island. We are not Whoville! The Raging Grannies, the Marxist Leninists, the disaffected, and the tax revolters may be out in force competing for the annual award of the Cup for the Most Churlish. "A waste of money!" they say. "What about the arts, health, the climate, the war, and corruption?" All probably true, but please, let's at least have a little joy. I was going to go down to the dock to watch the floatplane come in the harbour and cheer, but I'm afraid the protesters will just make me cross. I'm staying home, making jack-o'-lanterns for tonight and putting new batteries in my "singing fish." The pianist has made about twenty candy-coated apples with our label on them so the mothers will not worry about razor blades. What a world! The pianist thinks my singing fish might be scary but that's what Halloween is all about—All Hallows' Eve! The following day, All Saints' Day, the small children will continue to be protected and hallowed by the saints called parents.

The Tortoise and the Hare

This morning the tree men came. They scampered up a forty-foot-high plum tree that had many dead branches that thankfully could still be distinguished from the live branches as their leaves had not all fallen. The dead and dying branches are also identifiable by the growth of moss called Aaron's beard. That probably makes it acceptable for me to deal with the branches at my stage in life. I was impressed with the agility of the tree men and had initially worried about damage from large branches dropping on the rhododendrons under the tree. They took the heavy dead branches off in incremental portions and not a rhododendron was crushed. Then they did a tidy-up of some of the spent branches of very tall western red cedars. Tree-fallers and limbers rarely clean up the mess. They are high flyers! They finished their work in less than an hour and now the elderly eclectic gentleman has to cut up the debris with his loppers and tote it off to his shredder. It's going to take me two days. I enjoy shredding! I prefer to shred rather than burn the branches as it seems more organic. Cellulose gives body to the compost though it decomposes slowly. If you think this is a plaintive commentary, it is not. It's just to celebrate the contrast between the young and the old, the strong and the feeble. I can celebrate that! At the same time we all have our strengths. One of mine that I have learned the hard way is that time and patience will accomplish much. I can celebrate that as well! The tortoise and the hare!

Fauna Change

Today the Oregon junco has returned en masse to Lotus Island. They are slipping and flitting everywhere, exploring the locale. Next will be the rufous-sided towhees. They, like their cousins the juncos, are one of our winter birds. The towhees fly so close to the ground in the underbrush that I have momentarily mistaken them for rats. Startling! The black-tailed mule deer have lost their smooth caramel coats for a heavier grey-brown. The young bucks are starting to rut and have already slashed my declining Gunnera to pieces and soon they will sharpen their antlers on the bark of various defenseless young trees. The pianist and I watched a river otter run across the lawn to the harbour yesterday and it startled and flushed out a bunny. I don't really think an otter would harm a bunny, but the bunny obviously wasn't taking chances. The otter, with a long body and tail and short legs, runs in a sinuous, ungainly, loping fashion. The California quail walnuts are now large but still cling together and listen to mum and dad. There are a few runty fawns still around, late gestations, and I fear for them this winter as they have little flesh. In the winter there is often a corpse under the tool shed or the leaf piles. The deer here are endemic and as there are virtually no predators we have all adapted to the deer and they to us.

This is a great spider season. The webs in the morning, wet with dew, are fantastic and if you don't duck there is a risk of a face full of wet web. We are careful around the old rotting woodpile for the widow and the brown recluse. We finally took down a large empty wasp nest from the top of a pear tree; the wasps are long gone. The nests are beautifully made. The pianist put one in her wood-fired kiln and the clay base, when fired, gave us a lacy oval ceramic nest. The fruit flies in the fresh fruity compost generate at an unbelievable rate and it is not surprising that the ancients believed in spontaneous generation. Thank goodness the fruit is soon finished; it can be overwhelming. However, there is an interesting observation to make. Our own fruit in the kitchen fruit bowl has a myriad of fruit flies, whereas the supermarket fruit section has no fruit flies. Tells you something, doesn't it?

Homemade Wine

Today is Thanksgiving Day in Canada. It coincides with the Christian harvest festival. My daughter is a nurse and worked a twelve-hour shift last night. She will work again tonight, so her family, who usually come to Lotus Island for Thanksgiving, are unwilling to leave her alone in order to feast with us. Well, this time we will go to the mountain. The pianist and I are going there with the cooked turkey and all the trimmings. It's a bit complicated as their home is over the pond by ferry. Food transport of a critical warm mass is a consideration. Our daughter asked if we would bring some of our homemade fruit wine from the cellar. It's not rotgut, but it is not stellar either. I usually serve that wine with family, but why is it that we often take the people we love best for granted and don't always provide what we prize most? Why should we reserve our quality wine for the dinner party with friends who we like but do not love, and settle for less with some of the most important people in our lives? The answer to that is obvious. Because we can! Perhaps we should reevaluate where we put our "first fruits." It's kind of a useful question to pose as a Thanksgiving Day thought!

The Mixed Hedgerow

The hedgerow that separates our property from the beach was, to my knowledge, always there. All the hedge shrubs are indigenous to this area. They consist of snowberry (Symphoricarpos albus), ocean spray (Holodiscus discolor), Nootka rose (Rosa nutkana), big-leaf maple (Acer macrophyllum), red alder (Alnus rubra), and common hawthorn (Crataegus douglasii). We only remove the new growth so as to avoid disturbing the bird nests in the hedge structure. When this hedge is pruned annually or twice annually at four feet on the property side and twelve feet on the beach side it still has a look that belongs, rather than appearing cultivated. The diversity of plants, however, does provide a certain amount of chaos and the informality that a diverse population of people would also display. Plants with varying growth rates, both in time and season, variable production of flowers and fruits, both early and late, deciduous leaf colour changes and leaf drop at different times give a changing kaleidoscopic aspect to the hedge. The presence of a diverse indigenous mix provided by Mother Nature rather than a monoculture we might have provided gives a greater durability than we could achieve. I have resisted the temptation to monkey around with it. "Don't just do something, stand there!" has often been the best idea when facing Mother Nature's choice. The hedgerow, I think, represents the strength of the diverse population in a country like ours and especially a province like British Columbia, where strength, durability, and colour is present in all of its diversity. It just takes a little more work to manage than a monoculture.

Mother Nature's Fruits

The indigenous berries produced on the prairies, where cultivated fruit is rare, provided a wonderful bonanza in the fall: a gift from Mother Nature for the taking. I'm not talking of the cultivars developed from these plants by the plant developers at the universities and experimental farms, but the original plants that we harvested berries from in the olden days. Low-bush blueberries (Vaccinium angustifolium) from the Hudson Bay junction area. Your fingers were blue from the bloom on the berries and your back sore from the stooping. Your ears were alert for sounds of bears in the patch and your legs ready to run. High-bush cranberries (Viburnum trilobum) were from the same area but not related at all botanically or horticulturally to the common cranberry (Vaccinium macrocarpon). These high-bush berries made a tart and piquant jelly. The pin cherry (Prunus pensylvanica) also was a favourite for the jelly maker. A tart and delicious jelly was created, particularly good for meat and game.

My favorite as a child was chokecherry (Prunus virginiana). The flavour of jelly from this berry is unique. A slice of homemade bread slathered with butter and chokecherry jelly was ambrosia (food for the gods) from Saskatchewan! Because it took a long time to pick enough of these small and thinly distributed fruits, the preserves were special, a treasure trove, and treated with great care. The saskatoon berry (Amelanchier alnifolia) was widespread throughout the prairies. The berries made very nice pies and were easy to pick.

Saskatoons were the prairie icon, possibly less for flavour than ubiquity. The cultivars that have arisen as a result of selection have undoubtedly improved the production of these little trees but they will never supplant the fruit flavours one remembers from one's youthful taste buds. Mother Nature has provided indigenous fruits on the wet coast as well. We have abundant cultivated fruit on Lotus Island, so we often tend to ignore the indigenous offerings. Moreover, they don't compare to the prairie berries in variety. I don't include the Himalayan blackberry variants or the rowanberry because they are not indigenous. The trailing Pacific blackberry (Rubus ursinis), that little squirt that tangles everything you plant, produces a quality berry jelly, very different from its mellow Himalayan cousin. The salal berry (Gaultheria shallon) and the Oregon grape (Mahonia aquifolium) produce berries that our longtime neighbour used as a wild flavour addition to traditional jelly and jam preserves. The thimbleberry (Rubus parviflorus) and the salmonberry (Rubus spectabilis) are for the birds, and best left to them. There are many good publications on more of the wild fruits that may be worth trying. I can't say! Not in any way to derogate the abundant cultivars that are the anchor of the fruit industry, but it's worth trying a little of what our early ancestors had available to them, freely given, if only for the novelty. A paean to history and Mother Nature!

Agonal Bloom

In late fall as the groundwater rises and the light shortens, the dahlia patch enters the period of agonal bloom! The old plants have become exhausted, in part frustrated due to "seed production interruptus" from yours truly! Each time they produced a perfect bloom in order to entice an insect to pollinate it, the bloom was plucked. If it escaped plucking when prime, it got dead-headed well before the seed set. Now, in the approaching agony, the plant throws itself into a desperate budding frenzy to reproduce, to no avail! Feeble little curlicue stems, petal-deficient flowers, stem rot, colour-fading, nodding blooms, and a proliferation of unsightly "sports" are the end game. It gets scary. "To everything there is a season...a time to plant, and a time to pluck up that which is planted" (Ecclesiastes 3). It's inevitable, I guess, that we interrupt the natural history of the plant, or nature—or, for that matter, maybe ourselves—in order to produce other gain.

That's progress? Define gain. No one asked the plant if it wanted to stay and survive rooted in a spot that was drier in the winter and more clement. Or questioned the dahlia if it happened to produce some illicit seed from the pollen of a nearby dahlia colleague it fancied to create a new variety. Or forced to accept being pruned by a would-be exhibitor to one or two lonely stems for gain of another inch of bloom breadth and a millimeter of increased stem width. Or chosen to become the bride of a selected groom's family by a plant marriage broker, the bloom shrouded in a chastity belt after fertilization until seed production! Or it was allowed to flower 'til "untimely ripped" for a vase when in full pubertal beauty! We are digging up that which was planted in the spring on October 25 to solve the agony. The bulbs will be buried in a straw cloister for the winter and frustrated again next summer. In my hands they are always the bridesmaid!

Heritage Dahlia

Bishop of Llandaff is a heritage dahlia, first created in 1924. It is by modern standards very venerable, like its namesake. Llandaff is the Scottish Episcopal Seat in Wales where it was first developed. It cannot be purchased locally, but is available through friends, as is the one currently in my possession. My friend Sue, who gave it to me, tells of her parents' garden in Comox, BC, which was then a commercial rhododendron nursery but had some Bishop of Llandaff available. Her mother wrote to the Royal Horticultural Society in England to offer Bishop of Llandaff to them, since the society had written an article describing their loss of this treasure following the Second World War. They stated that the dahlia had disappeared in English gardens due to displacement because of the war effort and the priority of food gardens. The pianist tells me she believes her "nana" grew it in her garden in Regina as well. The plant is a small, semi-double dahlia with a red core and rich red petals. The foliage is green-black with small but attractive crenellated leaf margins. This is the only heritage variety I have, as most of the dahlias I own are modern hybrids produced by a limited number of committed hybridizers. The season this year has been exceptionally long and the dahlias are still in good bloom. I am looking forward to growing Bishop of Llandaff next year! A dahlia that has remained with quality morphology over almost eighty years and has an affectionate following among knowledgeable growers has outstanding worth. It may not have the lushness of today's varieties but it has character and history. A lot in life depends on which characteristics you prize!

African Violets

In May of 2007 the pianist and I celebrated our fiftieth wedding anniversary! Our daughter bought a large number of African violets for the table settings. They are still blooming for us! African violets are beautiful but fussy and if you are to keep them in good health the care is rigorous. We ordinarily couldn't be bothered maintaining plants that are not user-friendly, beauty notwithstanding. However, given the circumstances, these are keepsakes. Having a greenhouse and a potting shed is an advantage in maintaining houseplants during their rest period and the necessary pruning, splitting, and re-potting, but the real secret is care during the bloom period. The violets are the pianist's wards and she is as fussy as they are. They are bottom-watered and the leaves gently stroked with warm water. She maintains the plants by situating them with a good view of the east. They are fed lightly every ten days or so and unwanted growth and spent blooms pinched to extend the season. She does the same with the second-cousin of the violets, a Streptocarpus that was given by a good friend years ago and is therefore also a keepsake. We still have, after three-and-a-half years, most of the African violets and their offspring. I could never do this labour of love, since I am too impatient. Plants of a keepsake nature are nurtured not only because they are beautiful but also because they have meaning, history, and relevance to the ongoing relationships in our family. We can't take them with us. It's now or never! There is no potting shed in heaven.

Sunrise Lost

On Lotus Island at the end of September, the sun rises behind the cedars to the southeast, so we will no longer see it rise in the morning from our vantage point in the living room. What we will see is simply the dawn of a new day. We will see the sun rise again in late March. The wall of western red cedars buffers us against the November gales as they come in from the southeast, so the trees are a blessing. The harbour depth goes abruptly from the twenty-fathom mark to the seven-fathom mark a bit out from us, so the large rollers generated from the rise in the harbour bottom, along with the wind, are bracing. There is always interesting flotsam thrown up to intrigue the curious. A massive rock wall, piled to move with the waves, protects our bank. Those who flee to the desert in the south may be pleased to avoid the season's change and the rain and wind, but the pianist and I would miss it. There is something about the turn of season that signifies the reality of the temperate zone, its four seasons and its inhabitants. We belong! Getting through November to Christmas is the darkest time. The winter ducks, American widgeons and buffleheads, return through the winter, 'til April. They choose to come here. The widgeons are dabbling ducks and stay close to shore. The buffleheads are diving ducks and feed further out. They fatten up at the March herring spawn time to enhance their fertility and prepare physically for their long migration. The ducks don't seem to mind the wind and rain. The day in March that we see the clear view of the sunrise from the living room, for the pianist and me, is the hallmark of our new season.

The Altar Guild

I take great pleasure in the elegant displays of the altar guild women who, amongst other things, provide flower arrangements for the Sunday service. For the months of August, September, and October, dahlias are often used, along with russet peony leaves. The leaves are a great complement to the dahlia colors. When they pick from my dahlia and peony patch it is an honour for me that I share in the worship. I suppose in one sense we all have some sort of icon we use to center worship, in or out of church, but Jesus used all sorts of worldly examples, props, and referred to all sorts of contemporary elements to illustrate his teaching. I suppose there is a certain ego satisfaction in supplying flower arrangement for the services, but that beauty represents an act of love and duty on the part of the altar guild women: a form of worship combined with a sense of unavoidable pride. My orientation always leads me to see the arrangement as a first connection. We take so many things for granted in a church or any other organization that depends on volunteer labour. The people on the ground, doing the regular hands-on work as a matter of commitment, are the people who really make the organization work. Some of the most unsung of groups are in fact the connective tissue of the church. You only notice when they are not there and then it's a catastrophe. The care and skill of the arrangements provided by the altar guild are a reflection of their Spirit. Take the time to thank them for the beauty they provide, week by week.

The Green Tree Frog

As I was coiling up my hoses I heard the little green tree frog with his mighty voice summoning all or any females to his side. They are very cute. Telus uses them in their ads along with lambs and lizards gambolling about. My friend, a greenhouse man, puts them in his greenhouse, I suppose to eat the insects. I'm not sure that they are in the appetite for anything but a lady frog. Certainly those of other species, and our own, are not very hungry for food in a state of unrequited love. I never had much luck with my friend's greenhouse tactic. He told me he enjoys the frog music, but I found it was quiet when I was with my prisoner captured for the greenhouse. My transplanted frog in the greenhouse withered on the vine, as it were. I think there was pining and a wasting away because of unfulfillment. The rule probably is, "Don't muck about with Mother Nature too much." To employ a frog to do your dirty work eating insects in the guise of being organic is no excuse. Think of his feelings. He is a brief enough candle as it is, what with working for Telus, living in the great big world, singing, seeking and procreating, just surviving the environmental degradation to which he is so vulnerable. As you know, he is the canary in the coal mine. He won't live beyond his allotted life span outside the greenhouse but so what! Toiling in the workhouse is probably worse. Slavery! Too little to fight back. There isn't anything fundamentally wrong with a short but happy life of freedom. Sing "Let It Be"!

The Scythe

Last week my friend asked if she could borrow a tool to cut her long grass because her grass and brush were too tough and long for a weed eater. She said, "Do you have a sickle? I know you have a lot of tools." I don't have a sickle but I have a scythe. The scythe is not only an ancient tool but it ranks in importance with the binder and the combine in the march of agricultural harvesting technology. Nowadays, sadly, the scythe is not used much. I lent her my scythe and a stone. The important thing about the scythe is to keep it sharp. You can maintain a scythe's sharpness with a hand stone, but from time to time, if not used much, it needs a rotary grindstone. The stone has to be used in the correct way. It takes time to learn to sharpen the blade to make the job easy. No job, however humble, is simple. To cut effectively one develops a rhythm much like a golf swing, with the back stroke equally important to the cutting stroke. The swing becomes relaxing if you let the tool do the work! The blade of the scythe leads at a fifteen or twenty-degree angle from your coronal plane.

When I was seventeen and eighteen, I worked for the CNR as a section man for the summer in the Touchwood Hills. Our June job was to cut the long grass on the right-of-way. Five men would move along, each cutting the measured interval between two telephone poles, and then leapfrog ahead to the next available interval. After each cut we'd roll a cigarette, of course! The right-of-way has a downward slope on either side and we, being responsible for six miles of track, always cut on the downward slope, up six miles and back six miles. It took us two weeks. Once you got going in tandem there was some irregularity in smoke time, determined by the fastest man. Of the five of us, no one wanted to be the slowest man but after an hour the pace evened out. When you have six miles out and six miles back the only time you hurry is the last hundred yards or the last ten minutes in any day. I haven't seen my friend since she borrowed the scythe but I hope she enjoyed it. There is no finer feeling than a sharp tool slicing through long grass, which lies down in geometric windrows at your bidding.

Slugs

It's raining today, so it is a good day for dispatching slugs. They are staying out longer. I no longer use toxic materials added to solid bait as they are also toxic to furry and feathered friends. These chemicals were always highly effective and the liquid slug bait is still safe if used sparingly. The best organic method is to cut them in half; this is a rapid and humane way to eradicate them and leave them to recycle "in situ." We have blacks, browns, grays, and the ubiquitous banana slug on Lotus Island. If you tally your kills you will be able to assess the efficiency of your control mechanism. You can even plot the number killed against cutting days and come up with a nice bell curve if you are so inclined. Slug-killing methods are contentious here in Lotus country! An incredible fact is that even killing slugs is mildly contentious. That is because a zealous few see the active and ongoing digestion of organic material as nature's catalyst. Thank heavens they are not my neighbours! In respect to methods of execution, some advocate animal-friendly methods such as ferrous compounds. These are not toxic, at least in modest amounts. The crows here, however, eat ferrous pellets as soon as they are spread, as they look like seeds. The company doesn't tell you that on the package. Those with small gardens advocate copper wire or copper-impregnated fibre strung about the periphery of the garden. I'm not sure it works but if it does it would require constant adjusting. Various baited trap and drown systems are also available.

One year I collected a full garbage bag of hair from the barbershop sweepings since someone told me slugs would not cross over a hairy strip. I decided, however, that dandruff, old hair, and vegetables didn't go hand in hand! Since slugs will cannibalize the corpses of their fellow creatures of any stripe, half of a dead slug is the best bait for another slug. You can return with your trusty secateurs and slice the cannibal in half while he is enjoying himself. Two for one day! This keeps them occupied and away from your plant. Certainly, of the organic control options, this is the most effective, surgically satisfying, accountability-accurate, humane and consistent with good non-toxic recycling principles. It just means you have to get up early before they go under rocks later. My tally today was 110 slugs, including one banana slug.

The Botanist

The first year I was at the University of Manitoba the botany examination was a week after the rest of the final exams. To save money and relax, I gave up my boardinghouse room and took the train home for the week, intending to come back in time to write the exam. My dad was the railroad station agent so I had a train pass and my transportation was free. The night before the examination day, I stayed with my nanny and grandfather. I was ready to write. When I got to the university in the morning I found that the examination had been held the previous day. I was in a panic. I had misread the examination timetable. I had done badly enough that year despite my best efforts. Culture shock bewilders! Botany was my best course. I thought my putative career was dashed. Nanny said, "Why don't you phone the professor and tell him what happened? He's a nice man and he goes to our church." I called him at home, told him my circumstances, and left the stuff about my grandparents and church out.

"Well," he said when I phoned, "I'll write you a new test and you can come to my office for invigilation today. Mind," he said, "You won't get a really good mark." The relief I felt I can still feel today. Botany was a small class and he knew I was an interested student. My family and I were lifelong gardeners and I was also interested in the flora of the Whiteshell. The professor spent his summers tramping the lower reaches of the Canadian Precambrian Shield, of which the Manitoba Whiteshell was a part. Despite being in his sixties, he didn't differentiate between his vocation and his pleasures. They were one. It is the hallmark of a happy man. The blessing that kind man gave me was a precious gift. When you are as close to the edge as I was that year, the little things are important.

Currants

Someone once told me, or I read, that the Queen loved red currant jam and that the company that supplied her provided a few jars with the seeds handpicked out of the jam specifically for her. Red currant jelly, though delicious, doesn't have the wherewithal of jam. Whether this seedless jam is an apocryphal story or not, I am sure it would have been a "dainty dish to set before the Queen." Frankly, seedless jam would be too fussy for me. Get a toothpick! Our currants this year have an abundance of tresses on both the red and white. The cousins, gooseberries and black currants, are not berried in such abundance. I know of no other way to avoid currant maggot in these precious little fruits than carefully staged spraying with Malathion at flower time. There are wild currants and wild gooseberries on Lotus Island so the maggot is endemic. No amount of good husbandry will eradicate them, though with care you can minimize the damage. Slight infestation of currant maggot is like slight pregnancy. The crop is still tainted. If you label your jam or jelly product to state that you have used Malathion at flowering time, you ought also to say on the label that these currant and gooseberry products do not contain "essence of maggot"! Don't be dissuaded from staging three spray sessions of Malathion at flower time. It's a nuisance now since the "greening wave" has meant I have to travel to the agricultural outlets to get the spray. The nurseries no longer sell it. These four little fruits harken me back to my Manitoba roots with my grandparents. It may be that the Manitoba winters were often too cold for the currant fly pupae to survive in the soil. Those were the days without poisons!

Cherry Pie

Montmorency cherries are yellow-red sour pie cherries that are hard to find because the industrial processors buy them all. Stony Creek Winery in Ontario used to make a nice Montmorency wine. Some fast food restaurants have sour cherry pie turnovers but they are mostly glairy filling with red colorant. The Montmorency is much more reliable on Lotus Island than the Morello, which is red and prettier. It's still a fact that flavour trumps appearance, though the consumer sometimes becomes seduced by appearance. We have a productive thirty-year-old Montmorency tree and the birds leave the sour cherries (unlike the sweet cherries) alone long enough for us to pick them ripe. With the sweet cherries, the birds are voracious and eat them well ahead of ripening. Today I made several deep-dish cherry pies and cherry filling as well. The biggest problem with cherry pie making is stone removal. It is tedious, but the tedium can be lessened during the picking of the ripe fruit. If a little eccentric pressure is put on the fruit when you pull it off, it will leave the stone on the tree. A certain finesse and dexterity is necessary! Speed of processing is necessary as the cherry juice darkens (oxidizes) quickly once the stone is out. I always warn dinner guests to chomp the cherry pie softly since I always miss a couple of stones. You have to microwave fresh Montmorency cherries well, before you make the pie filling, since the fresh cherries don't cook down well unless pre-softened. Cherry pie is a lot of work! There is no way that charming

Billy Boy's intended could make or bake a cherry pie quick as a wink, talented or not!

Loganberries

When the pianist and I moved to Lotus City in the sixties, the adjacent farmland was dotted with loganberry farms supplying the fruit wine industry locally and the jam factory on Sinclair Hill. Now the jam factory is an unused heritage relic and the Logana Winery is converted to a heritage structure housing an upscale steak eatery. Soft fruit loganberry jam is available only from industrial manufacturers except for minor cottage industries. Grape growers and vintners, primarily large franchise holders, have displaced the local loganberry farms. This part of the world was prime country for loganberries and never was prime country for wine grapes. They produce pretty fair wines from specialized stock in this area but they will never compete with quality wine worldwide. We grow world-class-quality soft fruit varieties. Why don't we stick to what we can produce of excellence? Tastes have changed. Still, we could compete better in the long term with what we do best, not second best! I suppose we have to live with industrial farms and industrial food manufacturing. But hey, what the heck!

Yesterday I made thirteen jars of loganberry/tayberry jelly from our berries. I guess we are our own cottage industry. I missed the jell-point and bottled too soon so I had to dismantle the seals and reboil. It's a bit harder to jell loganberry juice than some fruits as the loganberries have little pectin. My grandmother and the pianist's mother never added pectin to jellies but they could assess the critical jell-point to the second. "Lightly jelled" was the mantra for optimum achievement. The industrial jelly makers always add pectin and chemicals. I also made twenty two-cup bags of loganberry/tayberry juice for freezing. The pianist makes a loganberry juice meringue pie after the manner of a lemon meringue pie. It's a delicious and pungent dessert treat. Loganberries and tayberries are easy to grow if you have room on your fence. It's satisfying to know you have a year's worth of eating from your own ground, by your own hand, in your own cottage, with sure knowledge of the contents!

Robin, Canadian of Course

Every day for two weeks the pianist and I watched the daddy robin attack the big window of the studio. He'd stand on the adjacent car's side-view mirror and stare at the studio window. I guess "glare" would be more accurate. Then he would fly at his mirror image, traveling up and down the window repeatedly, screeching as he flew. We thought he was crazy 'til we saw he was nesting in the kiwi bush also adjacent to the window. We moved the car so he couldn't see this apparent adversary. Despite us having moved the car, he continued to perch on the mirror but peered at himself upside down and pecked at and fouled up the mirror and the side of the car. He intermittently tires and gets busy with worms rather than fighting the phantom. Dear me! He has seen the enemy and he is he.

My neighbour is a car buff. He has robins as well and the behaviours are the same. He, however, "has no time" for bird shit on his cars. His ploy is to simply cover the side mirrors with little plastic grocery bags, securing them with elastic. It works, but his beautiful cars always look like they have a perpetual bad hair day. I look in the mirror from time to time these days and I recognize my shade. I have to deal with the taunting from the shade about my shortcomings, which, by the way, I already know. I'm not going to cover up the mirror to hide my adversary! I have to see and take direct action with my shade, including recognition! The robin adapted and busied himself with worms but I'm not partial to worms. Our fledglings have flown so there is no fledgling for me to protect. I suppose I should wash our car. Maybe I will write stuff!

Osprey

I have been watching the osprey fishing in our harbour today. They nest across the harbour by the Three Sisters islands. The water is deeper there, so the birds fish on this side, where the water is shallow and the fish are nearer the surface. At first sight the osprey appears to enter headfirst into the shallow water but comes up with the fish in the talons. Therefore they must make an abrupt turn at the surface of the water after the dive in order to seize the fish with the claws and surge up on the wing through the surface tension of the water. They are so fast at the turn you can't tell just by watching. The osprey is a beautiful bird and more adept at hovering and diving than the eagle, which swipes the water when it fishes. The eagle's technique is more in keeping with picking up ducks, its more usual fare. The osprey is far less commonly seen than the eagle in our area. Later in the season the kingfisher appears and fishes in the same spot as the osprey—hovering in the same way, diving in the same way but entering beak first and coming up with the fish in its beak. Hover and dive and breaking surface back into the air in one fluid motion requires strong wings, strong necks, patience, accuracy, buoyancy, and good knowledge of the best fishing holes! Both the kingfisher and the osprey are an object lesson in elegant ergonomics. An osprey picked up a fish today a short distance from my nose and right under the nose of a blue heron. Success in "one fell swoop."

Rhubarb, the First Fruit

Rhubarb is the first fruit of the season. Some say that rhubarb is infra dig. What a heavy trip to put on a beautiful and ancient plant! I think that comes from the fact that it is too easy to grow. They said, "If you can grow it on the prairies it can't be much of a feather in your cap!" Practical people have got out of the feather and cap business. Do what works! I think there is something of vegetable and fruit snobbery in the food business these days. People often want something exotic they can't grow or won't grow. With rhubarb, this may be because urban people don't have a big deep patch to plant perennials, or else have a limited knowledge of cooking from the garden. Rhubarb freezes beautifully with or without sugar. The variety I have is "Victoria" and it's easy to grow, provides a lot of product, is immune to disease, and is free of pests. It's a gift to the novice with a deep dirt patch and a good compost pile. We lift and split the roots every four years and replant in a different part of the plot.

The pianist and I make twelve to fourteen frozen deep-dish rhubarb pies in cake pans every year. Picking and preparation time is easy and rapid. Timing is everything for harvesting rhubarb as it quickly extends into currant and gooseberry season and the stalks decline here after June. I could never keep the rhubarb plump enough to combine it with our strawberries when they ripen. Some like the combination but we haven't tried. I suppose we could use California strawberries. The pianist likes the small stalks since her mother was of the opinion that the rhubarb sauce was redder. I like big stalks since they are faster to process. We work it out. There is nothing nicer than a rhubarb pie at Christmas for you and your children and grandchildren. When one is born on the bald prairie at the height of the Great Depression, one never totally escapes the dread induced in you by your parents that without basic food that you can grow or store you are somehow naked and exposed. Rhubarb gives you a big bang for your buck if you grow it yourself!

Squirrel Scraps

The little brown squirrel that is co-owner of this ground is not easily taught to clean up his mess on top of our barbeque. In the fall he spends a lot of time pulling off the scales on the Douglas fir cones and eating and hoarding the seeds, leaving the scales strewn about. Now he has clearly opened his storehouse of last year's maple tree seeds and resurrected them, cracking them open and eating the seeds, discarding the husks. Home for the little brown squirrel, according to my neighbour, was in our woodpile. Not the new one but the old punky one that we have given up on—the one that is slowly slipping back to nature with a mix of bugs.

Why does the squirrel store food in one place and then transport it up to our barbeque to eat under the barbeque cover? Maybe he prefers not to eat in the old woodpile now with all those bugs. It's possible that he has observed over time that the barbeque is our place to eat and he thinks to emulate us. I don't blame him. He is very social so maybe he likes company. He can eat and talk at the same time! He is very saucy too. He gives us the ole' eyeball as he eats and scolds, almost saying, "You don't frighten me, buddy boy! I can move like lightning if I want, skip and fly; I don't want to yet! So there!" I love his attitude but I worry because we have a lot of raptors that enjoy squirrel. What I find are the scraps he leaves behind, all the seeds removed, husks and scales littered about; he neither cleans the table nor wipes up after himself. His table manners seem atrocious.

I clean up after him at least once a week. It's worth it for us to be his buds!

Clam Digging

Today my neighbour and I dug clams. Actually we deep-raked clams, as they are only a few inches below the surface. Butter clams and littleneck clams are abundant on our beach since there are very few people that care to harvest them now. I don't know why that is since they are delicious in chowder, which I am about to make. I picked up fifty clams in a nine square foot area with about twenty minutes of work—if you don't add in forty minutes of talking time. I'm soaking them in water now to encourage them to get rid of the sand. I'll steam them up tomorrow in order to facilitate shucking and then make Manhattan clam chowder. The pianist doesn't like clams, so it's all for me. Once you start to collect clams there is a natural tendency to take more than you really need. Some restraint is good, only because you can get yourself in a mess cooking in factory-like volumes: chopping vegetables, straining the liquid, packaging, labeling, freezing, and washing up. Now that I think of it, maybe people are smart to avoid clam-digging.

This is the first week in three months that we have had daytime low tides. Despite the fact that my neighbour and I could never make a good living manufacturing clam chowder, it is a satisfying pursuit to cycle what we think is our own resource. Of course, calling it "our own resource" is nonsense. We return the shells and adductor muscles to Mother Nature's beach for recycling. In Canada, the people "own" the beach just to the high-tide mark. Forgive me for saying "own." It's only a manner of speaking. We really lease everything in this life anyway!

Garden Bones

The bones within the established enclosure we call the garden are dry bones and living bones. The mighty conifers, old orchard trees, and venerable ornamentals have "ruach" and are living bones. If they are well-placed it is unwise to disturb this skeleton created by Mother Nature. They carry their own sinews and flesh and lift them up as a risen testament to life. The dry bones are another matter. Notwithstanding Ezekiel, these dry bones will not rise again; they will not be covered with their own sinew and flesh and they are expendable. The thoughtful gardener will work with the living skeleton to complement its beauty and confine himself or herself to working only on the bed on which it rests. The dry man-made bones of terraces, latticeworks, fences, new beds, and structures can be changed or modified to suit the palate of the current garden custodian. One can add sinews and flesh to these structures but they will never grow sinews or flesh themselves. No mighty tree can be replaced within a gardener's lifetime. No birds of a variety will frequent your enclosure without trees. No sweet or otherwise songs will fill your air with passion! Your exhilaration in meandering will be muted. "Thus there are two books from whence I collect my divinity: besides that written one of God, another of his servant Nature, that universal and publick manuscript, that lies expansed unto the eyes of all; those that never saw him in the One, have discovered him in the Other."* There are an infinite number of shorter-term things you can do to put your own imprimatur in place on the page. If you protect the living bones and listen for the "ruach" you will be doubly blessed.

Religio Medici by Sir Thomas Browne (1643)

Cucumbers

I have been labouring under the illusion for years that gynoecious cucumber plants produced cucumbers without the need of pollen from male flowers. I assumed that the greenhouse growers never had to provide space for a male. Apparently that is not so! I am now given to understand that the seed sellers include a marked male seed or two in the package with the females. Cucumbers labelled as gynoecious have female flowers primarily but still need a pollinator male. This seems eminently more sensible; why didn't I clue into this before? I think it is because when I ordered seeds of Carmen, a cucumber that has performed well for me in the greenhouse, it cost about $2.00 a seed and there were only five female seeds in a packet. There was no male seed in the package! The answer, I learned, is that Carmen is a parthenogenetic cucumber! There is no male seed needed.

What we have in some plants, some lower-order animals (including bee varieties), and some experimental species could generate a crisis for the "drones" of the world. With the contemporary ability to modify genes at will, it makes us simpletons wonder who is the Creator after all. All we have going for us in sexual reproduction is genetic diversity, which guarantees (at least as much as any guarantee is possible in this uncertain world) the capacity for long-term adaptation. Asexual reproduction presents a bewildering genetic discussion in Wikipedia. Boys, you had better get to work to find your niche before it's too late! We probably will never get to the point where Mother has a talk with her adolescent girl about sex and the cukes and bees rather than the birds and the bees, but we are a little closer. Parthenogenesis! Moreover, the offspring of these cucumbers, Carmen, are all sweet females. Prolific and not bitter! Parthenogenetic: out of the woods, gynoecious: not quite out of the woods.

Witching

The phenomenon of mind–body interaction is mysterious. When the pianist and I bought our piece of ground on Lotus Island the first job was to look for water. We had use of a jointly owned well, but we needed a backup plan. We hired a witcher. There is a reason it is called witching. It may be more accurate to call it "bewitching." Moreover, I had seen the movie *Mr. Blandings Builds His Dream House*. I had some knowledge about the fruitless search for water from the dowser in the movie, which was not encouraging! Our dowser came with his witching rod of willow and dowsed on our plot in the most likely places. I expected the process to be amusing and primitive. Sure enough, his dowser dipped and water was found in an area near the surface. Actually, it was too near the surface to be of use, other than as a cribbed shallow well for watering the plants. We never bothered to crib it. However, I was intrigued about the mysterious process and started to dowse on my own. I tried forked willow, forked vine maple, and a wire coat hanger. If I approached a part of the lot where water was possible, each of my witching tools would dip easily and strongly, including the wire coat hanger! What was this phenomenon? I do not know.

As a scientist it is easy to be skeptical, particularly about other peoples' inexplicable experiences. One can say, "What benefit will accrue to this other person if they are convincing, or is it worth their while to fudge the truth?" Or one can say, "Is this other person sincere but credulous?" Or one can accept that there is a realm of phenomena for which we have no logical explanation. Speculation is not a substitute for explanation. I wasn't committed enough to drill several dozen holes deep into the bowels of our ground to investigate whether I was crazy or not. A mind–body phenomenon! It is seen in medical practice regularly, displayed by otherwise sensible people. I am convinced that though my mind said this was nonsense, my body responded as if it wasn't. I discarded the occult, recognized cognitive dissonance was in operation, and relieved the dissonance by connecting to very good municipal water.

Mother Nature's Garden

In the more bucolic parts of Lotus Island, Mother Nature's handiwork is in full display this spring morning. The Indian plum (Oemleria cerasiformis) is in full flower. This small tree or shrub is the first to flower here. The plum is widespread throughout the island and, like us, is not spectacularly beautiful but is plentiful, durable, and fruitful. The red alders (Alnus rubra) are abundantly present throughout Mother Nature's plot and the red catkins are in full bloom. Though the red alder is so named because of its red bark, the male catkins, when a grove of alder is seen from a distance, give a beautiful red-brown hue to the landscape. The westerly view from the Fulford harbour ferry is fantastic.

The wild American plum (Prunus americana) is also in bloom: white-flowered, beautiful, and abundant. It might be more of "an escape" than Mother Nature's wilderness baby. In a way, though, I suppose we are all "an escape." It just depends on when rather than whether! Over our painted deck the three western red cedars (Thuja plicata) have been dropping their cones for the last two weeks. The tiny cones stick to the deck because of their little irregular scale-like shape. They don't seem to provoke interest from the Oregon juncos that are making the rounds right now. "The air is thick with pollen," the pianist commented to me on our walk yesterday. It has to be the alders and the Indian plum, as the maples and cottonwoods are not in bloom yet. Last year's maple seed cases winged their way onto our shingle roof in the fall and have split and produced hundreds of seedlings growing in the shingle roof. I hate to disappoint the seedlings but the first few dry sunny days and it's curtains for them. Thank goodness!

Gumbo Soil

Life on Lotus Island does not include living with gumbo! The thin, stony, acidic loam of Lotus Island, with high drainage capacity, needs work of a different kind than the sticky gumbo of our storied past on the bald prairie. In the early spring before planting season in Kindersley your best shoes had two pounds of gumbo on the soles that wouldn't shake off when you came home from school. You had to use the mud scraper to get anywhere with gumbo removal. There certainly was a reason we had wooden sidewalks in those days (except you wouldn't expect a kid to always walk on the sidewalk). Here on Lotus Island, a mud scraper would be a foreign object of an unknown nature to anyone other than a stubble-jumping refugee.

The nature of the gumbo meant, of course, that a later planting season occurred on the prairies; it dried slowly, particularly if the snow load was heavy and the ditches and dugouts were full. That was OK for us since the soil had a better tilth when it dried a bit. Curiously enough, when we planted here on the wet coast in April and on the prairies one planted on May 24, by mid-July the vegetable gardens in the prairie towns were ahead of ours. Hot nights will do it! We didn't have running water in some of the towns we lived in but with gumbo soil you could get away without watering much, as a general rule. Not always, but the soil was remarkable for water retention. There was no contest from the wet coast for vine-ripened tomatoes, sweet corn, peonies, and lilacs. Gumbo soil, hot nights, and an unwillingness to give up water to the hot air was what it took!

Golden Bantam Corn

My brother Phil challenged my recollection about the sweet corn of our youth. He maintained that Saskatchewan had too short a growing season to produce a sweet corn superior to that of the wet coast. The pianist, who spent each summer as a child in the Qu'appelle Valley (Saskatchewan), swears that they lived on beefsteak tomatoes and Golden Bantam corn in the fall, grown in their valley cottage garden. She says her memory is as "sound as a dollar." These days that doesn't say as much as she intended about her memory. Golden Bantam was the "pièce de résistance" of the sweet corn family in those days of yore. It had a large stock with small irregularly rowed ears. It was no match in appearance for the modern hybrids, but so what! It was sweet, matured early, and you could save the seed. It's now a heritage variety. Phil is probably right that my memory is a bit tricky, as is that of the pianist. I am allowed, however, to be extravagant and embellish my anecdotes as poetic license. Everyone must know that sweet corn always tasted better when you were ten than when you are eighty. No ten-year-old worried that his cob had irregular rows and was unusually small, since there was always more where that came from. One of the great joys of reverie is the pleasure one gets from revisiting history through rose-coloured glasses. "Precious memories how they linger…" probably sung by more artists than most any other elegiac song. The past just seems like yesterday!

Bee Keeping

Over the years, kindly beekeeping friends have lent us hives for the apple orchard during pollen season. Honeybees are more reluctant than bumblebees to come out in cool weather, so conditions have to be right for them. My friend, an experienced beekeeper, has been supplying us latterly with two hives, which suffices. We get the pollination and he takes the honey. Our bloom is a little early this year. We usually figure May 5 for maximum bloom of the Gravensteins, at least the king blossoms. I am always in awe of the way bee experts such as my friend handle their jobs with such ease. I have had to call him for a seething and shimmering swarm hanging on an apple tree like a football, a bee colony in the crawl space of the house, and a bee colony in the hollow of the trunk of an old Transparent. Each time, he responded with skill and dispatch. The only time I was in danger of getting stung was weeding the strawberry patch when the bloom was good in the patch. We had a young family of friends visit us for tea and cookies last summer. The young mother cautioned her children to stay away from the hives. We have a tree swing and a climbing tree in the orchard away from the hives; however, the little boy couldn't overcome his curiosity about the bees and got too close. Then he gave the hive a little kick since there wasn't enough action that he could see. At six or seven you can't outrun bees. Of course he ran right by his sister, who was obediently on the swing. Their mother came barrelling into the orchard in response to the screams. It was chaos! The bees were in their clothes and hair. The children were hustled into the kitchen and stripped, where we picked out and squashed bees from hair, bodies, and clothing. The kitchen floor was littered with dead bees. The pianist ran upstairs to get the bee sting kit. She applied the sting stick to the spots. The children were fine and so was their mother.

After the initial shock there was relief and even a sense of having come through an event. The children were remarkable and suddenly became excitedly good-humoured. Adrenaline rush! I couldn't get over how resilient they were. It bodes well for their futures. Their mother experienced the "whew factor." Our forgettable afternoon tea transformed to an unforgettable afternoon. There was no allergic reaction to the stings, thank goodness. Maybe the adrenaline rush was curative. We are provided a wonderful self-sustaining body! I asked the bee man to remove the hives. The pianist and I are not going through this again! I'll rely on the wild bees.

Powerless in Paradise

The first major storm of November, with wet, heavy, sticking snow and high winds, has culled the rotten, the weak, and leaning maple and alder. At the edge of the forest they overhang the power lines. Peripheral trees and ditch-side trees crush the power lines from the awesome might of Mother Nature. She is dealing with the trees as the Grim Reaper deals with the old and the feeble. We were forty-one hours on Lotus Island without power, landline, Facebook, or all the other accoutrements we have come to take for granted. Mother Nature is no doubt going to repeat this a further three or four times this winter but the first big one is the major cull, much like the flu season. It was always thus! Global pruning! Wolf pack at the edge of the herd.

Our anxiety extended primarily to the two freezers in which we park our frozen, value-added fruit creations and frozen dinners, valued for the summer and fall work effort rather than monetary value. Our frozen preserves survived the forty-one hours since we scrupulously avoided peeking. Black November, source of SAD* for many. Cause of snow-birding for others. At seventy-six years, rapid dark adaptation with the older eye and heat transfer from the body core to periphery is not what it used to be, so dark and cold is dark and cold! We had lots of wood, rock salt so we wouldn't slip at the woodpile, and both the fireplace and the Vermont Casting were going full blast. As long as one rotated the backside and front side it was bearable, but reading by candlelight is tough; by flashlight it's hard on the arm. We don't have miner's lamps. Hibernating under two duvets and a blanket, nostril to toes, was the real ticket! What was good about all this, however, was the incredible silence and the sense of power in self-sufficiency that one gets from knowing that we are all in the same boat and making do. Unlike our forebears, we knew it would all end. I am ashamed to admit the payback pleasure that was obtained by knowing that our children were worried about us. Still ducking the widow-makers in Paradise! Still salting the slippery slopes!

* Seasonal Affective Disorder

Mold

Mold season is here on Lotus Island. Mold always seems to get a bad rap but "it ain't necessarily so"! It's also the season for spiders and mold's fungal cousin, the mushroom; both are also subject to bad raps. The only reason fungi grow on anything is because they can. Get rid of the substrate and you'll get rid of the fungi! In the meantime beware of badmouthing the molds. If it weren't for Penicillium notatum we wouldn't have developed the range of subsequent generations of antibiotics, and many more World War Two survivors would have succumbed to overwhelming infections without the first-generation antibiotic. We wouldn't have Stilton cheese to go with our port! We wouldn't have truffles to lighten our wallets.

The chrysanthemums in our foundation boxes are on the way out with mold. The grey mold may not be beautiful but it is doing its job of assisting in biodegradation. That is where it's at with Mother Nature! Certainly mold does not have the beauty of the mushrooms my Facebook friends are posting today. If the mold on your tea rose, or your wall, or the green fuzz science experiments in the back corner of the fridge, or your basement, or on uncovered tomato plants is a problem, it's not Mother Nature's problem; you're the problem by providing a substrate mold will thrive on. If the mold you wish to grow thrives on what you provide for it, you will also thrive. It's a curious paradox that the genus that can kill you can also cure you. The genus that can tear you down can also build you up. Here's to the mold family, beautiful and homely!

Homegrown Vegetables

Growing home vegetables is usually a bust. The cost–benefit ratio in the hands of the home vegetable gardener is a disaster. I like to say, "I spend ten dollars to grow a dollar's worth of vegetables!" I am aware that this point of view will spur fury amongst the committed: the seed catalogue producers presently mailing their coloured pictures and their devotees. They will accuse me of egregious incompetence but I have to come clean. I have tried my best off and on for forty years. I have read, studied, and inwardly digested the books of the great vegetable gardeners and tried their techniques. Arthur Willis, Bill Vander Zalm, W. G. Smith, Dr. D. G. Hessayon, Jill Severn, Bernard Moore, and Marjorie Hunt. I have subscribed to Rodale's *Organic Gardening* and various Ortho publications. All to no avail! I have grown everything from salsify to stevia, from peas to potatoes. The occasional success is not worth the effort for me.

There is a solution to getting the great taste of homegrown organic vegetables that will cost less in the end. My daughter has organically farmed vegetables for twenty years but it is hard work. She is exceptionally knowledgeable and can make a living but it's a tenuous thing. She does it because she loves it and sees safe food production as an essential in the "food world" that is spinning out of control! Lotus Island has a salubrious climate that allows both winter and summer vegetable growing, but it is also kind to many of the pests: carrot fly, leaf miner, cabbage butterfly, cut worm, a myriad of fungi, rabbits, slugs, sow bugs, and earwigs. Water-logging, tomato blight, unexpected frost, and a sorry lot of other enemies combat you. If you love it anyway, then bring your Remay, your fibrecloth, your little collars for the cole crops, and your lumber for the raised beds. Bring your compost and your slug bait and Rotenone. Not me! I'm sticking to rhubarb and globe artichokes in the vegetable category and growing ornamentals. We'll buy our vegetables from the organic marketers. It's easier on the budget and we won't need "Hope springs eternal." She can stay in Pandora's box.

Pee on Your Compost

My friend Earl told me years ago that his prospective in-laws, who had never met his parents, came to visit them unexpectedly at their home. The old boy was out, said to be turning his compost pile, and the enthusiastic visiting mother-in-law-to-be volunteered to get him and rounded the house only to catch him taking a pee on his compost pile. Since he was an Englishman he raised his hat to her. What else could he do? I was relating this story to my family as I thought it was funny and the pianist said to me, "You've never done that, have you?" She looked at me through querulous eyes.

"No," I said.

My daughter said, "Yes, he does. I've seen him stand and pee on the compost." You can rarely get away with anything in a family! I told this whole story to my friend Ez'. I excused our behaviour based on the fact that both Earl's father and I lived in an area of Lotus City that was private and secluded. Ez' lived in a wealthy enclave of Lotus City that was less secluded.

I said, "You, on the other hand couldn't get away with it because your properties are more open. Your neighbours would see you."

"Yes," he said, "that may be true but my neighbours have too much 'je ne sais quoi' to say so." Touché!

Crum Jelly

We have a forty-foot plum tree (Prunus cerasifera) that is an "escape" from somewhere. It is a red-leaf plum that produces an abundance of small, one-inch, somewhat sour red plums in such abundance that the birds cannot keep up with them. I probably collect fifty pounds of plums and boil them down for the rich red juice of superior color. There is, however, little or no pectin in these plums. But, serendipitous as it may seem, the pianist and I also have a mature Dolgo crabapple (Malus domestica), from which we collect a great many crimson crabs and boil them down for juice of a similar rich color. I have been doing this for decades. The crabs have lots of pectin and when the two juices are combined for jelly-making a very superior, piquant jelly emerges. This is Crum jelly, the family favourite for bread and for meat. I hang the boiled fruit in the basement from the rafters in big cheesecloth bags that I make from bolts of muslin. The boiled mash drips overnight. The scene may appear grotesque to some in the semi-dark. Years ago, my little daughter came screaming upstairs when she looked in the semi-dark basement. Her elder brother had told her we had butchered and hung our white Samoyed and it was dripping blood. She thought he was teasing her but peeked into the dark basement and fled at the sight! Forgiveness sometimes needs a long reach.

The Church Bazaar

This morning the pianist and I are taking our culinary efforts to our church bazaar. The prospective purchasers are certainly of a highly discerning nature when it comes to the culinary arts. I have tasted a sample of the pianist's products. They are brown sugar meringues with walnuts and pecans, and a flat cake loaded with flaked pecans. Delicious! My product is Dolgo crabapple jelly that has great color. My jelly is in jars that I haven't sampled recently so I am taking a chance. It usually is saved just for the family so it doesn't matter if it is hard-jelled or lightly jelled but now that I'm into the quasi-commercial racket the pressure is on; it has to be just right! I suppose it is pride. Since it's been stored for a short while and was just intended for our use I had given short shrift to cosmetics. Now that I am going public I needed a cosmetic upgrade. I washed any sticky bits off the lip sides of the jars and polished the brassy lids for presentation purposes. I removed bits of ancient prior labels that I had previously ignored. The cosmetic was what I was hanging my hat on since I took a chance in not testing the content again. I carefully labeled the jars with new stickers in my best printing, which does not measure up to the pianist's hand. I've done my best.

I appear to be the only male providing a product in the food division. I seem to be the only member of the food division with primitive printing on my labels. They'll probably say, "It's OK, he's just a man!" I hope if I have to take it all home again I'll be able to buy back my own product. I can't rely on the forgiveness of the public for accepting the excuse that "he is just a man." I don't want the forgiveness of the public by accepting the excuse that "it's just the church." I've had an epiphany and that's what church is about, after all. I've forgiven myself and I'm buying my jelly back early in the morning so I don't need to forgive anyone else for saying "he is only a man."

The Wet Coast

This is monsoon season on the wet coast in the Salish Sea. We have had a solid week of heavy rain and wind and there is another week of the same to come. Lotus Island is soaked through and through and the water can merely traverse the surface of the full sponge. The tides are high during the day so with a southeast wind and a flood tide the waves are rolling and pounding against the rock wall. All decked out in rubber rain gear I look like Captain Ahab on a bad storm day. Living on the seashore is a weather experience. One is always aware of the ocean's presence. Luckily when we had our builder construct the house he made sure the underground drainage piping was placed in critical lies to carry the water away from the foundations. The pipe boxes need to be checked and cleared from time to time to prevent silting up. Water does not flow uphill and we live in the shelter of the Hundred Hills. This wet weather is a boon for the rhododendrons and the western red cedars. They had been stressed by the long hot and dry summer, particularly the cedars, which showed a lot of leaf death. We are experiencing El Nino ("the Boy"), arriving with the warm, wet, windy weather of the early Christmas season. Some call it by its secular name, the Pineapple Express. A wet is a wet, by any other name, a wet. In a world that is frequently suffering from lack of water most if not all of the time, we should be thankful for large mercies and minor inconvenience.

Winter moon

The full moon is small and silver tonight. It looks like a winter moon and appears to be moving rapidly through the grey drifting clouds in the blackness. It seems early for a winter moon. The tide has been out at night here on Lotus Island for the past month but it has not been my inclination to dig clams then. I like to make clam chowder with tomato sauce and lots of chunky vegetables. We have abundant littleneck and butter clams. The pianist is not keen on clams so I do it for me. I'm waiting for daytime low tides as it is difficult digging under a torch. The moon is too small to cast a good light and it's cold out on the beach in the dark. November really kicks in with dark nights, wind, low tide, clam chowder, fireplace, and pale silver winter moon riding the dark clouds. You have to take November by the neck and shake it to get rid of the doldrums. Probably the brisk winter winds will drive out the doldrums by allowing one to spread one's sails and fly! There is nothing like energy to get your wind up to banish them. The winds push you forward, flush out lethargy, give new oxygen, and tingle and burn your skin. Beautiful summer days are easier. Lovely fall weather is exhilarating. I need to work at November to make it more palatable.

Peony Leaves

It's curious how often a visible sign is a reminder of an invisible presence. Now that fall is here, the peony leaves are turning a russet-red and beige that melds with the still vivid dahlias! They remind me of our friend, now departed, who first suggested this combination to produce the spectacular flower arrangements she routinely produced for the Altar Guild. The peony leaves are of such a colour in the fall that the entire spectrum of dahlia colours read with them. They belong together! Our friend was an elder of our church and had sung for almost fifty years in choirs. The pianist acted as her church ward when she became significantly confused over the latter few years before her death. She never lost her discerning eye, however, for an incompetent flower arrangement. Moreover, she was always able, to the last, to read music and sing the complicated choir arrangements with considerable skill. As long as the pianist ensured the hymns were prepared for her in sequence, the pages turned for her, and a guiding finger identified the line from time to time, she sang like a lark. What interesting software we have for a brain that allows a savant area, retaining our favourite and valued aspects despite the failure of the rest. I never walk by the turning peony leaves without a moment of thought that like them she will sprout again to grace a new altar and sing a new song!

Garden Party

My oldest and some of our dearest friends came over to Lotus Island from Lotus City to put my garden to bed one weekend in October of 2001. That year I had broken my tibia in July and it had not healed by September. The plates and screws immobilising the fracture had broken and the screws extruded. The fracture was freely mobile and progressively angulating. It was re-operated on in September, bone-grafted, re-plated, and re-screwed. I was six months non-weight-bearing in a three-wheeled electric scooter from July until Christmas. I was able to do some gardening from the scooter but it was pretty limited. One of my friends planned and organized a work party of a dozen old friends with whom we had many adventures. They were a group with which we had hitherto often celebrated Halloween weekend at our friend's country home. The party came with tools and zest and worked like Trojans, cutting down the spent perennials, cutting down the Gunnera, raking, blowing, and hauling an enormous leaf fall from the big-leaf maples. They buried a deer discovered under the leaf fall during the rake-up period. Work included covering the Gunnera with three feet of leaves for the winter and filling the compost bins. It was like the old-time barn raising.

I was on the scooter and raced from pillar to post giving free advice, exhilarated by the help. I needed to do something without getting in the way of good work. The pianist capped things off with a big turkey dinner and liberal libation. I can't remember a time when I was more touched than by this good-natured and spontaneous act of generosity from my friends. It may seem strange that in the midst of my limb disaster I would be so happy but I was. At the end of it all I graduated to crutches, partial weight-bearing, and became "right as rain" by the spring. That was the best garden party I have ever been to!

Harrow my Roadway

We have a small gravel driveway on our bucolic property and it has compacted over time and become pack-ugly. The fine material comes to the top and the three-quarters-inch stones descend to the nether. The fluffiness is lost as well as that wonderful crepitus we hear greeting our return as the wheels move over the loosened gravel. A gravel driveway lends itself to better traction when wet as there is less slipperiness than in a smooth driveway surface of any material. However, the structure of the pack-ugly roadway is lost in a picture of homogenized banality and adopts the physical characteristics of the smooth-surfaced applications.

My neighbour has a garden tractor and a coil-spring-loaded harrow he purchased from a catalogue. He harrowed my driveway and parking area with considerable skill, giving rise to artistic circles and undulating harrow marks reminding one of a Zen garden. The theory is that the three-quarters-inch stones will, with repeated harrowing, rise to the surface after the loosening of the packed powder and small stones. The first rains that arrive will drive the powder below the larger particulate matter and give rise to a renewed, bold, formed structure of gravel. Physics 101!

My neighbour is a master of tractor control and wove his way like an artist as I watched with admiration. His price to do this work was some earthworms (for trout fishing) from my rhubarb patch. I was anxious to retain the center grass down the driveway that adds to the gumboot essence of our hidden treasure; he skilfully preserved it.

I look forward to seeing the end result following the monsoons to come on the wet coast. The artistic pattern will go and like all beautiful events will have to be recaptured. Zen again and again. I hope I don't run out of earthworms.

Pruneophobia

This dreadful disease can render the aging Homo sapiens inhabitants confined to a jungle cage of green by the house, stooping at frequent intervals to avoid hitting their heads. One sees them sweeping their arms constantly in front of them to advance through the tangled web of branches! The light gradually dims and the view disappears. The wet becomes wetter! Animal droppings increase and if you don't step on them from below they drop on you from above. The house windows eventually become sealed over and the vines penetrate your house siding and enjoy the interior warmth. The plants no longer have to fruit or flower since reproduction is low on the agenda for the vegetatively unrestrained. They don't need to be fruitful.

I confess pruneophobia has always afflicted me. The pianist and I have a continuing issue over this matter. I have avidly read self-help books on pruning to cure my condition but I still debride plants in a surgical manner. Pruning and debridement are not the same. Gardening on the wet coast consists of controlling things from growing. Gardening on the bald prairie consisted of encouraging things to grow. Surgical debridement of plants would consist of removing broken branches, diseased branches, crowded ingrowing branches, dead wood wounds, and drainage of pockets of debris. That comes naturally to me. Shortening something to fit or cutting to encourage fruiting, flowering, or branching is not part of my surgical lexicon. It seems anathema to me and yet I know, down deep, it's necessary. I still get anxiety if I have to cut for non-debridement reasons. If the saw or clippers cut through normal tissue I hear a small still voice that says, "Are you doing this for me, or you?" If a patient asked me that, I could cheerfully affirm debridement was for them. It appears to me now that pruneophobia, despite my surgical indications, is a touch of garden madness.

First Nation's Spirit

It has become increasingly apparent that the First Nations in this country often have deeply felt spirituality and equally deep appreciation of their roots. Despite troubles and frustration, they have remained planted and deeply rooted. Such is hardship that it gives birth to expressions of continuity with the Earth and the Spirit! This continuity they retain provides leadership that a fragmented and increasingly secular world has lost. They have a new strength and the Spirit is moving amongst them. They are unabashedly celebrating the Spirit and the roots they have taken ownership of. It is uniquely their own. There is a resurrected willingness to proclaim a heritage that was undermined for centuries. There is not always blame in my mind for the past injustice that was perpetrated on the First Nations since it was often out of ignorance rather than malice on the part of our "white culture." We can really never walk in ancient shoes!

Cultural genocide, ignorant or evil, is a darkness, by any other name a darkness. The current move to forgiveness the First Nations are providing us is a blessing, but we should never forget! The strong sense of a coming together of First Nations seems to have gained a momentum that will hopefully grow like the snowball down the hill. What a turnabout! The former Indians to whom we proselytized in the olden days have now provided a new, strong, and needed example of spirit and unity as an example to the rest of us. We also have much to give them. Would that we would speak and listen!

Maple Pole Bean Mania

Cobble Hill Ruthie and I were talking bean stakes yesterday as she was having trouble finding suitable ones. Her pole beans are now up. I told her I used fresh-cut maple sapling shoots. They grow all over Lotus Island on the edge of the roadside ditches and are now eight to twelve feet long. They are perfect for that use and they are free! If one is careful while cutting the shoot at the base so as to not disturb the cambium layer at the cut, then when one uses a dibble to make the holes to anchor the saplings, they will root at the buried node since they have the force majeure protected. One must have planted a node with the germinal root cells well below the surface of the dirt. When the shoots are first selected and cut in the ditch, one may seem a madman to the vehicular traffic as it whizzes by on the road at eye-level. By spring, the shoots are branching in the ditch from all the nodes so each branch is trimmed to an inch on each sapling for the subsequent purchase of the bean stringers as they grow.

The pole beans I use are Blue Lake, for no good reason other than I always have. These plants are heavy but they have strong positive thigmotropism and could cling to a pig-greased pole; nevertheless, it is best to have augmented the support with the one-inch branch purchase points which will help the bean shoot curl tightly and hang on. A good homemade dibble is an old broom. Drill a big hole six inches from the end of the handle and shove in a long bolt of matching size through the hole. Leave the worn-out broom on as a lever. Your foot on the bolt plunges the dibble into the dirt and if you use the broom as a lever you can wiggle your dibble. Stack the maple shoots around your bean sprouts and bind them together high up like a tepee. There are a lot of pluses to these maple stakes. As the stakes begin to root, the beans begin to climb with considerable celerity. The weight of the beans causes the flexible cane to bend, which tightens the bean stringers. The lateral stringers tighten too, so the bean-sapling unit becomes taut and therefore strong. The rooting capacity from both bean and sapling roots provides a firm foundation. The rooted maple sapling sucks up nitrogen but the bean is a nitrogen fixer and so pays it forward. Isn't Mother Nature wonderful in her symbiosis?

Success in human nature can take a lesson from the bean-stake unit: strong, flexible, rooted, teamwork, paying forward, bean-counting, and self-sustaining. Bean pods stand at head height, where the air is clear and the sun is bright. As I thought about Ruthie yesterday, I also thought about Jack and his mother and his cow-for-bean enterprise. I have an interest in plant sounds, especially beans. Listen closely with each ear! Batteries charged so one can hear! Trill but soft, a little thrum! Fee and Fie, Foe and Fum!

The Three Sisters

This morning the Three Sisters islands in our harbour are backed by dense fog and so look like floating islands, discreet and resplendent in brown and green. They are unimaginatively named First, Second, and Third Sister and are mostly uninhabited since they have no potable water. They are not parks, but we treat them as such for excursions to what is called Chocolate Beach, which is on the Third Sister. The beach is a favourite spot for novice tourist kayakers. For the pianist and me, it used to be seven hundred pulls of the rowboat oars to cross the harbour to Chocolate Beach. The beach is composed of fine tide-deposited ground seashell as the islands were used as a Salish aboriginal gathering place for shellfish processing in the long-distant past.

Chocolate Beach is not named for chocolate candy, but for the chocolate lily (Frittillaria camschatcensis) that grows there. The Salish First Nations used the bulbs as a food source. Woe betide anyone who picks this protected species now. Our kids, in the past, explored the islands, since there were several haunted squatter's shacks at one time. Now we have no kids, there are no shacks, and we only watch.

Since we have moved toward renaming the Gulf of Georgia "the Salish Sea" we could give the Sisters more romantic Salish names in keeping with their centuries of use. George the Third lost some of the Gulf Islands to the Americans in settlement after the Revolutionary War. Given that fact and his miscalculation, I think it reasonable that we change the name of the Gulf of Georgia, along with these islands, to names reflective of the original inhabitants. John Ralston Saul, in his most recent book, *A Fair Country*, makes the point that Canadian identity is greatly influenced by aboriginal healing circles, justice, and mediation. Maybe we need to acknowledge that by having the Three Sisters renamed by our First Nations, since they were important to them as a home away from home and food resource and have little significance for anyone else!

Apple Surplus

When we have surplus apples, as we commonly do, so does everyone else on Lotus Island. What to do? The Community Services have a glut of donated apples. The deer are still available for handouts! There is a shortage of their preferred food in the fall and I am not about to plant things that they enjoy. It's a perfect use for the apples as long as the deer balance their diet. I used to spread apples on their customary pathways but feeding troughs keep the place a little neater. The troughs are under cover so the apples don't drown. After a while they contain lots of deer slobber and grotty bits. The deer don't seem to mind. I have just cleaned up and blow-dried the area and will pull the troughs back under cover.

In the past I have composted old apples and they add a lot of speed to the rotting process. We also make cider in the summer, in volume, so there is lots of apple and pear mash for compost as well. I am still troubled by "waste not, want not" so I avoid being agitated through using these useful alternatives for surplus fruit. We never fully outlive our backgrounds. Growing up on the bald prairie, apples were in short supply, particularly during the war. My brother Ken, age five, stole an apple from the grocery store in Kindersley. My mother sent him right back with the apple to apologize. That was a mistake! The grocer, Clem Reid, said to her, "I told him, if he was going to steal an apple, he should steal a good one." I don't think that my mother was satisfied with the grocer's admonition. She resorted to the hairbrush.

The Past is not a Foreign Country

David Lowenthal wrote a book called *The Past is a Foreign Country* in 1985. It's a wonderful book describing history, memory, and reliquary, amongst other things, plus the desire to relive or collect the past. One of our daughters, two of our granddaughters, and the pianist and I made apple cider yesterday from some of the Gravensteins. We made thirty quarts of juice heated to two hundred degrees to pasteurize. Our press is a sturdy thirty-year-old hand-crank, and our routine is long-established. The design of the press is probably hundreds of years older. The mash is great compost. We have a country kitchen and we press on the grass just outside the kitchen door. This link to the past is lived by us today in a real sense. The software we call a brain somewhere has a Facebook page that records part of my father's farm and my grandfather's orchard. It is indelible and structural. My granddaughters, as sure as the sun will rise tomorrow, will one day press their own apples in their own orchard.

Yesterday, as well, we went to an old folks home after church. Some residents are blind or have short-term memory problems but they respond to the singing of the old chestnuts that we sang in the church in years past. The pianist plays the piano for the hymns. One of the hymns they love best is "In the Garden." The garden is one loss always grieved by oldsters living in institutions. I love the song too, primarily since the funerals of both my mother and my dad had this hymn at their request! The old folks have intact long-term memories.

So do I! These linkages to the past are, for me, evocative of the connection with my grandparents and my parents. I do not long for the two-holer or the town pump or the kerosene lamp, nor do I wish to see one. But I don't believe the past is entirely a foreign country.

Fall Season

Fall is my favourite season. Gravenstein and Cox's Orange apples are ready to harvest and press for juice and pies. Pears—Anjou, Bartlett, Clapp's Favorite, and Conference! Transparent apples are put away in pies in early August and Northern Spy and Red Delicious for keepers come later. The summer heathers are still hanging on and the split leaf maples are changing into riotous colors. The bigleaf maples, indigenous to the west coast, provide great compost material, and we cover the Gunnera with the leaves to prevent frost kill and make leaf mold. The dahlias are in slow decline but the chrysanthemums have taken over, and what muted but beautiful colors they have. We don't always spray so we have some scabby fruit that composts beautifully as well and reacts with all the shredded branch prunings that provide cellulose to the compost mix. The hawthorns are turning leaf-yellow with reddening haws and look like a gorgeous shawl. The Dolgo crab has been picked for juice and will be mixed half and half with the wild cherry plum to make what we call Crum jelly. The pile of the summer's compost is out of the bin, which is empty now except for its starter layer, ready for this fall's new compostables. When I was young and strong I used to haul seaweed up for compost: sea lettuce shed in June and eelgrass in October; I am too feeble to do this now. The quince don't ripen 'til November here and they often crack. I haven't been able to solve that. The rhodos have made it through the very hot summer with frequent watering so there is no further need to do anything 'til the spring. I have more than enough to do to bother heading them and they are too big. I suppose I should if there were enough hours in the day. Stone fruits don't do well in my hands. The peaches and prune plums produced well for fifteen years and then have rapidly declined. The Japanese plums bloom here in March, which is too early for the bees except for a few bumblebees. We have a lot to think about here in the fall. It's easy to get fragmented. I guess, as our parish priest once said in a sermon, "the mind of God for you is to always do the next necessary thing." The pianist and I assemble ourselves early in the morning, with several cups of coffee, to decide on our day and reckon whether we are really doing the next necessary thing!

The Exhibitor

My dad was a good gardener and loved to exhibit the results of his efforts. The garden club's motto in Lotus City was "Share what you know and show what you grow." He gardened there in his retirement and was an avid member of the Lotus City Garden Club, but he had mellowed by then. He and I often gardened together when I was a boy in the olden days living on the bald prairie. He grew up on a farm and had no training in horticulture, but he had the knack, in spades! His exhibiting on the prairies started with sweet peas and vegetables; he grew sweet peas on a single stalk for the longest stem, the most florets, blemish-free. He grew cucumbers that were perfectly straight, sweet, evenly green without a flaw and big—but not too big!

Exhibiting and competition were everything to him. We exhibited gladiolus and dahlias in specialty shows in Regina, Calgary, and Winnipeg. His whole energy went into getting the biggest and best of specimens for the show, starting in the early spring. In our little town, the farmer, whose field we used, ploughed the gumbo soil with added cow manure. The freight-shed floor in the railway station where we also lived was covered with gladiolus corms and dahlia bulbs: corms that we had peeled, disbudded, dusted for thrip, and positioned for straight sprout growth. There was hardly any room left for the freight. I remember once driving to Regina all through the night in a truck with a load of glads, all staked, tied with rags, sitting in washtubs, stabilized through chicken wire. Regina was 120 miles away and I was not allowed to drive more than twenty-five miles an hour or the glads would shake too much on the gravel road. He drove the car in tandem, with all the paraphernalia needed for display. My mother went with me and kept nudging me to keep me awake. Going to Calgary or Winnipeg he could take his flowers in the baggage car because he had a railroad pass. He went to no end to compete! I, and most of my brothers and my children, inherited his knack. It is no surprise to me, however, that I am totally averse to exhibiting. My garden is personal. We take what we will from our parents and leave the rest behind.

Tree Crop Failure

This spring on the wet coast has been unusually moist for prolonged periods and the tree fruit crop on Lotus Island is almost nonexistent. I see a pitiful apple crop on the Gravensteins, Transparent, and Red Delicious. Cox's Orange has nothing. The Italian prune plums are completely free of any fruit. Same with the Damson and Victoria plum though they don't perform well for me in any year. In their case I suppose I should follow the Biblical suggestion: dung the plums for three years and give them the heave-ho if they don't produce. The early pears have some fruit as they seem to tolerate the wet a little better. Clapp's Favorite is early as it caught the warm weather in the two weeks of April and has some fruit but Bartlett, Anjou, and Conference have less. They bloom later. A few Montmorency cherries are present. We never get the sweet cherries because of the birds. I'm not whining about all of this since the processing of that much fruit is a lot of work and now I don't need to feel guilty about wasting the product. All the small fruits are doing OK and that will keep us busy. There is no shortage of bees at the moment since the weather has now turned, but too late for most of the bloom! I don't blame them for not working in the rain. I understand they don't really care about my apple appetite. It is just that I need them because apple pollen is somewhat heavy for the wind and the bees lug it from the pollinator trees to the Gravensteins. Just relax and give it a rest!

Weeding and Squatting

Weeding for prolonged periods in a fully flexed knee position, particularly with strapped kneelers, is dangerous. Popliteal artery occlusion, peroneal nerve compression, and thrombophlebitis are all reported, particularly in Asian literature. I thought of this yesterday as I was weeding my permanent strawberry patch. It is a flat patch in the grassy orchard and Mother Nature's plant invasion, designated as weeds only because of their location, are a tough little bunch. They consist of various grasses, as well as plantain, dandelion, daisy, knotweed, speedwell, and clover, along with the hit-men, bindweed and quack grass. I'm sure it is easier weeding to have an elevated strawberry bed or strawberry rows, but one needs to set aside space for this. There is always urgency to weed early enough to interrupt the seeding of these weeds. I will probably, after this patch crops, and in the late summer, dig the whole works up and select and replant the best plants. In the meantime I avoid a prolonged deep knee bend by going to another job every half hour or so, but it is darned hard to get up from the deep knee squat. I carry a burden of rectitude by using elbow grease rather than herbicides to deal with the unwanted. Some of the unwanted make good compost and the grasses can be used here and there to stamp into bald spots on the so-called lawn. The so-called lawn is mixed grasses so it doesn't mind added variety. So, I vary my workload, don't stay too long in this squat position, and know that kneeling for short intense periods is good for the soul as well as the strawberries.

The lady and the Gardener

Dr Y was an old-time doctor who was a member of the establishment in Lotus City when I first arrived in the 1960s. In a moment of utter madness he had purchased a large old Tudor mansion on acreage in the high-end district of the city. It was a beautifully landscaped property and he did the gardening work himself rather than hiring help as the rest of his neighbours were wont to do. He gardened in baggy cast-off trousers and an old slouch hat. Pruning, spraying, weeding, applying mountains of fertilizer and mulch—he toiled in the soil with his customary efficiency. A newcomer to the district and a neighbour seemed to take a particular interest in his work habits and eventually she came to Dr Y's fence and hailed him. She said, "I've noticed how you work and wondered if you might consider working for me as well. I'm close by. What do you charge?"

He thought for a moment and said, "The standard amount, but the lady here feeds me lunch."

"Oh," said the newcomer, "I can feed you lunch!"

"But," he said, "The lady here lets me sleep with her!" I don't know whether it was the slouch hat or the dirty baggy pants, but that seemed to bring cessation to the negotiations. It was said that despite the perhaps infelicity at the time, they became good friends and enjoyed a laugh. It is, however, likely that she was hesitant to become his patient.

Random Width Siding

A longstanding technique of cladding houses on the wet coast is board and batten. Houses built one hundred years ago have this application of vertical siding using cedar boards with the joins overlapped with vertical battens. Random-width boards are achieved by cutting the boards and battens from the diminishing widths of the entire log. As a result there is less wastage of the log. The appearance provided by the randomized widths is pleasing and the randomness is not obvious at first glance. It gave me a sense of having provided a green contribution with respect to maximum utilization of materials.

When we took down the cottage and built our house in 1995, the architect and the builder had the use of thirty large Douglas fir and western red cedar trees felled from our property, skidded off to the sawmill for eight months. The logs were custom-cut for the timber frame, the two-by-sixes, plus the randomized siding and battens. We had the length of the siding and batten custom-cut as well. I was an innocent in building matters but loved the idea of using our own wood. They like to say, in houses with large picture windows, "The design of this house brings the beautiful outside INTO this house!" In this case you could say as well, "The design of this house brings the beautiful outside ONTO this house!" Probably there was no real cost saving, but the idea of recycling your trees from the little plot into the house imparted an aura of romance. The trees never left home! That this matter of cladding used a time-honoured tradition and British Columbia's unique wood resource was for me an authentic expression of my song. There is no place like home!

Crow World Revisited

Three ravens visited our plot this morning, prompting a collective pursuit by the crows who really own the place! The ravens (Corvus corax) appear to produce extraordinary rage on the part of the crows (Corvus caurinus). The crows do not seem to mind the eagles, herons, or seagulls, though they do maintain distance. However, there is something about the ravens that always produces a noisy pursuit. The crows have a congregational lifestyle and the teamwork they display is remarkable. They always have a watch bird and a distant early warning system to alert the pianist and me to the presence of their enemy. The crows play frequently, diving and wheeling and rotating with one another at regular intervals. Life for them is not always serious. The raven tends to be a more solitary bird and seems more of an outsider, largely unwelcome by our birds. Unlike the raven, the range of vocalization of the crow is rather outstanding though I cannot tell precisely what they are saying. Certain phrasing seems consistent in certain identifiable situations. They have learned from the seagulls how to crack clams by dropping them from a height onto the rocks and they have no trouble competing with the gulls for shore-side delicacies.

I think the seagulls are too stupid to learn anything from the crows. The gulls appear to have no time for one another and though they congregate they are always competing, in contrast to the teamwork displayed by the crows. The crows know precisely when the smaller tree fruits ripen and they preemptively eat them completely two weeks before ripening, thwarting the now empty-handed orchardist. I wonder at the choice of the Stellar's jay (Cyanacitta stelleri) as the provincial bird. They do not have any skill or "savoir faire" to compare with the northwestern crow. They may be beautiful, but they are noisy, obnoxious, and have attention deficit disorder. I frankly cannot think of any bird that could compete with the brains of the crow. It seems "beauty before brains" was the operative phrase when a BC committee made the unfortunate choice.

Dinosaur Rhubarb

The Gunnera at the moment is resting under leaf mold. In the summer, it is "arresting." At mid-summer time the plant is ten feet tall with four-foot-wide leaves and our patch has a spread of forty feet and growing. Now, at rest, it lies covered and dormant in a bed of mixed leaves—its own plus maple and plum leaves. It takes me and my helper a whole day to rake, blow, and haul leaves to cover it in the fall. Three feet of leaf covering is needed as Gunnera is tender and damaged by a sharp frost. The leaf covering will compost down over the winter and the wonderful shoots will push the rotted leaves aside and emerge in the early spring. The growth of this plant is phenomenal if given the ample moisture it requires. It has been in its current spot twenty or so years and will take over our garden if I let it. I had it in another spot in the garden for about eight years and when we transplanted it to this spot I needed an excavator to move and plant the three monster root balls. I have not investigated the underground stems of this plant but Brian Minter, on his radio show, described the need for a chainsaw to cut them. My variety is Gunnera manicata. They say it may be eaten and is used for food in Brazil, but I am dubious. The deer, in rutting season in the fall, see it as a challenge and will savage some of the leaves. I don't mind, as it is starting to decline by then and it diverts the bucks from attacking the dahlias. I never bother to fertilize the Gunnera as it is buried in rotting leaf mold. The plant is large, coarse, spectacular, tropical, and in your face. It is probably a man's plant.

Beach Walk

Some foolish magazine has said Kitsilano beach in Olympic City is the third sexiest beach in the world. Yo! Not to take anything away from Kitsilano, I went for a walk on our beach today. I hadn't walked the entire mile of beach for at least six months, but the tide was out and it was a dull and somewhat windy day with a little west coast drizzle. My walk was sexy. There were three river otters playing and cuddling and watching me about fifty feet from the shore. They stick their little heads way out of the water because they are curious. I think two of them were pups. There were over a hundred Canada geese eating eelgrass. Some of it may have had remnants of the herring spawn from March still glued on. Mm mmm good! There is a sand bank of geoducks and if I touch the siphon gently with my foot to tease them, they give a big squirt! One lone eagle flew across the harbour and two turkey vultures cruised the shore. The wind was pretty brisk so they had updrafts. The sand banks have periodic congregations of sand dollars in the millions, but so far they remain very localized. The oyster beds seem diminished to me, but there is still a large oyster collection on the outcroppings of shale that dot the beach. They are Japanese oysters since we no longer have indigenous oysters here. I see someone has built a large and attractive house on the beach down the way. I hadn't seen it before. There was no one on the beach throughout my walk until I arrived back at our beach stairs. A young woman and a dog on a leash walked by, but she averted her eyes. Training, I guess.

Bee Cradle

Some of the honeybees "overnight" on selected flowers. Sometimes a flower's anatomy provides a quality petal cradle adjacent to the bee pantry. The bees are choosy where they sleep! Jomanda is a ball dahlia that has smallish upturned edges to the petals that are form-fitting for a demanding bee body and suitable for an overnight retreat. It also keeps them close to the pollen larder. They are worker bees so they don't have to go home at night to a mate, but just have to bring food home in the daylight. If they don't bother going home, they can start working in the early morning, which is admirable in the eyes of the workaholic, though I have found them a bit sluggish at 6:30 this morning. I roused them but they only showed modest enthusiasm. They left a few minutes ago and the cradles are empty now except for a messy dropping or two. We've always had hives until recently and I think these are escape variants that Mother Nature now harbours in some sort of tree hollow or wild dry refuge. Whatever! They are welcome here and perhaps have escaped the possibly mite-vectored disease, colony collapse disorder, that has assailed so many of their colleagues. While we celebrate their hard work bringing home the bacon, we know fresh air, sunshine, and freedom from crowding is the answer for them, and for all of us! We are also less likely to succumb to colony collapse disorder in that environment.

Organic Food

There is no doubt that food grown naturally is good for your organs. The organic movement has, through common usage, co-opted a word that I think in the olden days would have been a misnomer. An organ is either a musical instrument or a part of one's anatomy. When I grew up in a small village in Saskatchewan, everyone had a vegetable garden. The only amendment, as I remember, was manure, and because it was prairie gumbo, the dirt was always deep and required little watering other than initially after seeding. There were no chemical fertilizers or pesticides I can think of, other than Paris Green. What we grew we ate and canned, or at least my mother canned, in glass sealers. There was no plastic. There were no snap lids. There were no freezers. In a sense the organic movement is archaic, a throwback to my time and earlier.

The pianist and I went to the farmer's market yesterday and bought the most beautiful vegetables, full of sweetness, naturally grown by slim, healthy, bronzed people. What a pleasure! My daughter is an organic farmer and I understand the work entailed in growing that sort of food in a scrupulous fashion requires a diligence we never had to provide in the olden days. Certainly there were pests and plant diseases but they were far less numerous, as I recall. When one is largely confined to eating what one can grow, the palate becomes limited. When you have been through all the eating styles and limitless choices over seventy-five years, your palate may eventually return to foods limited by choice to those locally grown. Though organic food grown locally may, of necessity, cost more than that at the supermarket, we are so lucky to be able to return to food that is good for our organs.

Michaelmas

The Michaelmas daisy, which is really an aster, is a blessing that blooms in the late fall, in time for the Feast of Saint Michael and All Angels on September 29. My daughter, who lives nearby, gave me a clump of her asters several years ago for a vacant spot. What a colour complement in that season to the chrysanthemums and split leaf maples! I have a number of planter boxes adjacent to the house. I ruthlessly removed the rangy summer-blooming flowers, snapdragons, lobelia, and alyssum, and replenished the soil with compost and planted chrysanthemums and daffodil bulbs together. Two birds with one stone! Hopefully the chrysanthemums will bloom till mid-December and the daffs will carry on in February. The town boulevards on Lotus Island are alive with colour in the fall from the annual chrysanthemums and the red oak trees with their spectacular leaves, a welcome prelude and antidote to the winter drabness.

The holly berries are now turning deep orange so they are on the way. If we want holly for Christmas we have to cut it by December 10 because the birds eat the ripe berries after that. It's a curious thing that my neighbour has a hybrid holly hedge loaded with berries that the birds never eat. Our blueberry bushes have started to turn red early this year and we still have a final pick available since they are all bird-netted. My big job over the next few days is to get rid of the old raspberry, tayberry, and loganberry canes and string up the new vines. Routines like this give one lots of time to ruminate and talk to oneself. I hope my lips don't move! The garden is still alive at Michaelmas. It takes a rest at Christmas!

Bad Ideas

I idly thought of a potential treasure trove for the enterprising in recycled hair: human hair from the barber shop, pet hair from the groomers, even chemical hair from the beauty shops, dandruff and fleas notwithstanding, all collected from daily floor sweepings, gone tonight and hair again tomorrow! Think of it: the volume to be collected from all these emporia, free for the taking by someone with a broom and a bag. The rain forest on the Pacific coast in which we live is shared by the ubiquitous slug that forages on our vegetables and flowers. There has never been a satisfactory method of control short of making rounds early in the morning, dividing them in half and waiting for the cannibals to come so as to snip them as well.

An axiom in medicine: there is an inverse relationship with the number and variety of treatments offered and their effectiveness. Copper wire, beer, liquid and solid ferrous poisons, and endless barriers and pathway impediments are to no avail. Give it some thought: a tiny berm of hair surrounding the tender line of tiny vulnerable shoots which the slug would have to traverse, slug-slime coated in floor-swept hair, impeding every movement and dragging the creature to its demise. Think of it. A pickup load of hair from the multiple "Emporia of Victoria" each day to distribute to the gardens. I was enthused. Then I had a dream that hairy slugs entered the spinach patch and delivered hair and dandruff for the organic gardener's spinach salad. I had another dream that a realtor was discussing our garden as Hairy Acres. In my dream the property was impossible to sell. There is no end to fantasy and bad ideas.

The Fertile Mind

Harvesting from the soil over time without adding to it ends with depleting fertility and leaving it without muscle or synapse. Soil, like the mind, needs regular feeding to reproduce the fertility it was blessed with. Good compost may be likened, in one's life, to the fully digested product of past material experience. With water, air, heat, and those harvested materials from the past, a fungal, bacterial enzymatic biomass is created which will raise the composted materials into the fertile dust of renewal. The renewal takes time, heat, the right enzymes, destruction of pathological bacteria, the turning over of the compost, aeration, watering, catalytic admixture, and earthworms, which will tell you that you are on the right track. Is the remediation of the infertile mind the same and as simple as the compost pile? Maybe not, but I have to give it a shot, at least as hard as I work at the compost bin. It seems to me remediation of the mind is equivalent to the remediation of the dirt. Then you can trust that the ruminant harvests you have brought up from your past will be re-digested with care and with luck your muscle, muse, synapses, and mental fertility will be fulfilled and cause new growth in your life. We aren't that different from the compost. But both of us are special. We both came from dirt and to dirt we shall return.

Turf the Old

I observed during my times visiting our son in Scotland that the beech tree (Fagus sylvatica) does not shed its previous year's leaves until late in the following spring despite the cold winter temperatures in Europe. The beech hedges, widely distributed in Scotland, retain the browning and yellowed saw-toothed leaves through the winter, in contrast to almost all other deciduous trees, the leaves of which conveniently and expeditiously retire to the turf in the fall in order to make way for the young leaf growth in the spring. The old beech leaves are much more stubborn about going and need the young bud growth in the spring to expand and force the old leaf from its tenacious foothold. The elderly beech leaves serve a minor purpose, I suppose, in that they winter over and thereby increase the winter density of the hedges and moderate the wind. However, the appearance of the winter hedge is reminiscent of elderly gentlemen whose role is come and gone but who won't depart! Eventually, the youth will push them out and fulfill their role in providing continuing life to the plant. Because the old are reluctant to leave, the mess to clean up after their departure detracts from the work to cultivate the new growth in the spring. Why don't these old leaves go quickly in the fall like all self-respecting deciduous oldsters and give additional vitality to the compost over the winter as well as space for the new buds? Providing good compost for the young is the only duty of the old! I wonder if this question is horticultural or philosophical. They are the same! Aristotle says, "Nature does nothing in vain." It is incumbent on us, then, to consider that Aristotle may still be correct and therefore our need arises to seek to understand Nature's reasons. William of Ockham said, in effect, the correct answer is usually the simplest answer. If we believe that Mother Nature is always wise, then there must be a good reason that the beech is true to its nature. It is tempting, perhaps, to say the leaves stay on to protect the cottage-dwellers from cold Scottish winds, parenting and sheltering, as it were—but that is a benefit, not a reason. If you have any romance left in your soul you may consider the willingness of the young buds to avoid dispossessing their old from the perch into the cold turf before their time, dried up and withered though they may be. Compassionate nurture by the young buds, as it were. I like to think that Aristotle, Ockham, and Mother Nature would be sympathetic to that romantic point of view.

Lotus Island Spring

March 17: I was buzzed by a bumblebee today! As well, the pianist and I counted fourteen harbour seals clustered together: four lazy swimmers circling about and ten stationary swimmers "treading" vertically in the water, sharp little snouts looking skyward, all waiting for the spawning herring to appear! The Indian plum is in full flower and the Alder catkins are a cloud of red-brown. The bufflehead ducks are weaving in and out of the cluster of waiting seals, taking their share of the small minnows the seals ignore. The raspberries and loganberries have started to leaf and the rhubarb is poking up through the leaf mold. The gooseberries and black currants are leafing out but the red currants are a little behind. The apples don't have any green on the leaf buds yet but the pear's flower buds are swollen. The late storm surges over the last few days have thrown up an abundance of seaweed and have sucked out a lot of loose winter vegetation from the shore shrubs. This detritus has mixed together and harbours all the tiny denizens of the shore that feed the gulls and crows. The ground is like a wet sponge with all the rain, and the moss is especially thick this spring, giving a yellow-green luminosity to the canvas of Mother Nature lying supine before us in the sunlight.

I saw the little red squirrel today scampering about and he (or she) allowed me to approach within four to five feet, which is pretty good. They are quick, but I worry because the eagles are starting on the hunt in earnest, feeding bigger fledglings. There is green, green, green everywhere on Lotus Island today and since St Patrick was of the green, it seems right. We haven't been diverted yet from the green by the vibrant colors that will come in abundance in another month. Even the daffodil blooms are still in the anteroom. The greens are restful and as holy as St. Patrick! A serene sort of vibrant. I think I'll toast the green with a Black Bush or two today!

Formication and Slug Fest

The tent caterpillars are now dropping like rain from their webs after the feeding frenzy, having denuded most of the soft-leaf trees on Lotus Island. They are now resting for two weeks on any object they fall on, including the unwary. As they fall on the neck or head or clothing of the passerby they perform jactitations, swivelling and squirming here and there, giving rise to sensations of formication that linger in one's mind into the night when one wakes with the distinct but erroneous sense that something is still crawling on the neck, limb, and trunk. Imagine the bizarre tactile hallucinations of the psychiatric patient afflicted with symptoms of formication and their desperation to sweep or swat what is not there. The orchardist, working in the tattered remains of his apple orchard amidst the insect drizzle, has this phenomenon to look forward to as he sleeps fitfully through the night. Soon the worms that survive will cocoon 'til the middle of July and then emerge in force as yellow-brown moths.

The rain forest of Lotus Island has also bred a profusion of slugs this year; they munch the vegetation below in concert with the caterpillars munching the vegetation from above. I wondered if somehow Nature colluded with them to work in cahoots. This ground feeding is especially vexing to the gardener of iris and dahlia. However, during the early morning and nightly visits to the garden, the gardener, who must divide the slugs in half with sharp secateurs as he weaves his way through the rain of caterpillars, umbrella in one hand and secateurs in the other, is engaged in the most humane yet satisfying of pursuits. Chopping and squashing the small bodies of the slugs and caterpillars that ooze out the green juices of the gardener's vegetation is, I suppose, retribution. Tossing at night in bed, waking myself from a dream world of squirm and slime, is their revenge!

Dormant Spray

Luckily, we are beginning February with six sunny days in a row on the wet coast here on Lotus Island. It is warm and dry enough, and that's what counts for spraying fruit trees. Light wind has meant that the sulfur and oil will not blow back in my face as much as usual, but still, you can't spray with the pressure hose sprayer without some personal drenching. My glasses get repeatedly covered with oil and sulfur so I feel a little like—and look like—Mr. Magoo, fumbling his way around the trees. In the past I had to climb my twelve-foot fruit ladder to spray because my hose pressure then was much less, and the oil on the slippery ladder made the job even more interesting. I wear a mask, so my glasses fog up from the inside as well from heavy breathing and it's hard to clean your spectacles, front and back, with slippery, oily, yellow-orange hands. At least I'm not twelve feet up the ladder now. I always remember with terror a patient of mine whose foot and leg slipped between the oily rungs of a ladder; he turned upside down, fracturing his femur, and remained suspended by the broken leg trapped inside the ladder, hollering bloody murder. A cautionary tale!

I didn't dormant spray last winter, and it was much to my dismay when I saw the number of tent caterpillars and egg cases later that year and recalled the scabby pears and apples and the powdery mildew in the summer. Sulfur for the fungus and oil for the worms. In a sense, it is not unlike the preventative practice of medicine! Bad medical trade-off—femur fracture for worm prevention. I also see a lot of particularly thick black and green algae on the wooden deck and on the cement aggregate patio as well. There appears to be no end of things that I can squirt. I will also spray these areas with anti-fungus and anti-algae compounds and then power-wash. There is fungus, moss, and lichen on the roof shingles too, though they are not so bad. Spraying the shady side of the roof is also on the agenda before it rains again. What a battle with Mother Nature this week, but I am girded for it and the only downside is a monster orange ring around the bathtub every night, regular change of yellow underwear, and plenty of soap to get rid of the grease. If you choose to live in the rain forest, expect guests: Rain, Warmth, Pests, el Nino, and the Friends of Rot! I can say without fear of contradiction that there is a tide in the affairs of men that making hay when the sun shines is seizing the day!

The Un-heavenly Host

And there came to Lotus Island in the year of the Dragon, the un-heavenly host, Malacosoma, the western tent caterpillars, targeting and ravaging the soft-leaf trees, devastating the landscape throughout the island. I am still reminded of the drought years of the forties as a little boy on the bald prairie in southwestern Saskatchewan, with the grasshopper clouds eating every grain and leaf in sight, leaving so much bodily debris and grasshopper juice on the grill and windows of the Model A that it was difficult to travel. They even constructed grasshopper screens for the grill in those days. The windshields looked like a deluge of tobacco spit from the spittoon. The repeat worm plague that came on Lotus Island in a way resembled the plague of locusts in old Egypt and Kindersley from yester-millennium and yesteryear. The tent caterpillars on Lotus Island have now left the trees, since it is June and they are in cocoons, to undergo metamorphosis into the adult moth form in mid-July.

There is, I am happy to report, a glimmer of light on the horizon, at least on the patch of ground of the pianist and the elderly eclectic gentleman. I took apart and examined fifty cocoons on my blueberry patch. The cocoons are of an intricate construction. They comprise an inner sack that contains the headless black nymph, awaiting transformation from Cinderella to princess. This cocoon is a secondary oval silken sack, finely woven and close-ended. The outer cocoon is a loosely woven primary sack designed and spun initially by the worm to secure the later finely spun inner sack to the leaf and branch.

I investigated fifty compound sacks yesterday. There were only five sacks containing a healthy, black headless nymph that would transform to a moth. The balance of the sacks (forty-five) contained dead or immature nymphs in a state of dissolution, empty sacks without exit holes, or unidentified parasitic larvae foraging on nymph carcases. There were no gestating nymphs in a state of advanced metamorphosis. Today I see the devastated trees are beginning to re-leaf and the meagre ten-percent cycle-survival of nymphs suggested by my admittedly short and local series still gives me some cause for optimism that the plague cycle has peaked. I may be dreaming in vain, but unlike Joseph of the multicoloured coat, I cannot interpret a dream. I can only hope. Nevertheless, I am heartened to remember that when Pandora's amphora was opened, we know that Hope still remained available in the jar, while the ten thousand Evils spread their wings and flew out into the world.

Tent Caterpillar Egg Cases

The tree pruner came the first week of January and did a nice job of the apple trees, pears, and the Dolgo crab while listening to music through his earphones. He does the big trees, which are standards, and I do the smaller trees as I am now forbidden by my family to climb up my twelve-foot fruit tree ladder. About eight to ten percent of the one- and two-year growth on the apple trees have tent caterpillar egg cases this winter. I think we all knew then that an infestation was going to happen this coming summer since the moths, Malacosoma, were extensive in the past summer on Lotus Island. We are yet to have a sharp frost, which I am still hoping will do some pest destruction. Rigorous pruning will get rid of a lot of the egg cases. Dormant oil sprays will deal with some of the egg cases that are left as well, since the eggs need air. Brian Minter has recommended three winter dormant sprays but I struggle to complete one or two. The pear trees are safe; the leaves have a harder finish so the moths avoid egg-laying on pears. These caterpillars may be somewhat controlled on my apple trees with this shotgun approach, but the alders, birches, ocean spray, Rosa vulgaris, and wild cherries are also loaded with egg cases and I can't prune the whole countryside, so in the end we are going to have to rely on Mother Nature and the organic spray Bt* to interrupt the cycle along with the tachinid wasp. Though I have never tried Bt before, I am going to do so this spring. The trouble with Bt is the larvae hatch in graduated stages over six weeks here, so multiple sprays are needed.

The pruner is a nice guy, but leaves his cuttings for me to pick up for shredding or burning. Thank goodness I've help who does the bending and hauling with me while I do the shredding and burn what I can't shred on the beach. Shredding, I am sure, will destroy the egg cases when I compost the chips. Burning will certainly do it! Pruning, hauling, shredding, composting, burning, and spraying, spraying, and spraying. It's probably no more cost than a good gym membership and relatively as useful for fitness, but played to a different rhythm.

*Bacillus thuringiensis

Tent Caterpillar Moths

On Lotus Island the massive hatch of tent caterpillar moths has happened this week, the second week in July. They are everywhere, resting on the house siding and windows in hordes. Heat-seekers invading every cranny and nook where a little more warmth and light can be found. This spring was a moderately bad year for the caterpillar tents on the apples and other soft-leaf trees so the moth invasion portends a much bigger year next year. Interestingly, I had made a search the past winter for egg cases and found few, so concluded that I didn't need to dormant spray. Big mistake! The trouble with Lotus Island is the "green movement" is so driven that even dormant spray is considered by many a dirty pool. This spring I spent a long time cutting off all the tents on my trees and drowning the tenters in the harbour but I can't spare the time to drown the whole island population of caterpillars. Now we have to await the natural control mechanism by parasitic wasps. The tent caterpillars this spring, when observed, did not have that telltale dorsal white spot just behind their heads. I should say the satisfying white spot. The parasitic wasp has laid its egg there and on hatching the wasp larvae feed on the caterpillars. The rise of the worm population provokes a rise in the wasp population. Since the wasp larva has a specific need for that sort of food, as the tent caterpillar population declines, the wasp population eventually follows suit. Isn't Mother Nature grand? In the meantime, look next year for denuded springtime trees on the island due to the hatch of the massive number of egg cases that will come this fall and winter over. Fortunately Mother Nature provides a secondary leaf recovery. If you have apples, plums, and cherries, prepare for the worst! The tree can survive well without fruit but not without the energy produced by abundant leaves. Mother Nature is both grand and wise and looks down the road!

Scatological Investigations

The varied and colourful droppings of the ubiquitous northwestern crow are a useful source of information about the eclectic nature of their dietary habits. For those of us with a scatological bent, the seasonal changes and omnivorous habits of this species, Corvus caurinus, are worthy of outlet study since they are one of the most adaptable of birds, their success based on diet and opportunism. The pianist and I, living as we do in the country on Lotus Island, have the fortune, or misfortune, of having a large painted deck under three mature western red cedar trees that serve as a table-toilet for crows. The volume and character of the droppings from both tree and anus change remarkably through the season.

As I clear the tree droppings on the deck and its furniture daily with my gas-powered blower, I observe dry small cones, lichen, and moss fragments, arising somewhat from the crows' disturbance and the little red squirrel scratchings, and the seasonal needle drop. In the spring, small dead cedar branches are ripped from the tree by crows for nest repair and often dropped or dismissed for being unsuitable. When I have rid the deck of tree detritus, I have the opportunity to investigate the associated scat and sticky food leftovers, clam shells, half-eaten cherries, and red plums that have slipped through their toes after being pinioned on the branch. Naked cherry and plum stones, flesh successfully eaten in full, the scat from a diet of clams and tube worms, small birds or baby quail, sweet cherries and wild plums, pear and apple fragments: all leave a colourful digested deposit of crow scat—brown and crunchy, smooth or particulate, black and punctate, white and thin and watery—all with interesting textural variety and compelling graphic intricacies within the scat splat, Rorschach-like in nature. All scat pockmarks the deck with remarkable tenacity, resistant even to the gas-powered hose sprayer and requiring a stiff brush, elbow grease, and spray to remove. Even the glass-topped table and patio chairs are scat targets and all varieties are equally adherent to the glass and metal. If you are willing to pay the price for clean, pristine, aseptic eating on a deck under spreading cedar trees in crow and berry territory, you will never resent the blow, spray, and brush activity. Between the scat and the copious water spray, the cedars are secondary beneficiaries for the role they serve as a table-toilet for our feathered friends. Symbiosis: tree to crow and crow to tree.

Lilacs

While one can admire the dedication of the French hybridizers in the development and selection of superior cultivars of lilacs, there is a homely side to the old-timers of yesteryear and even more so the lilac root stalk progenitors. Syringa vulgaris may be seen in their varietal splendor at the Royal Botanical Gardens in Hamilton, Ontario as the pianist and I observed when we visited some years ago. They advertise "The largest lilac collection in the world." Despite Lotus Island being in rhododendron country, lilacs have a place everywhere as they are a ubiquitous presence. Every barn and abandoned house on the more sheltered prairies and the BC interiors had a hardy old-timer, surviving after a fashion without demanding a great deal of care. Maybe not as varied and fancy as the new grafted cultivars, but a survivor to be admired, with a touch of class; they added colour and fragrance to a sometimes drab environment. I have two lilacs that are grafted specimens and despite horror from the fanciers, I am withstanding the pressure from them by allowing a limited growth of the root stalk suckers alongside the cultivars! Though I treasure the cultivar, the progenitor is the creation of Mother Nature rather than the French hybridizer, and it reminds us where both we and the sucker developed from and what we have become, for better or for worse.

We should never forget our rootstocks and it works best if we still remember and harbour them. It's like having Grandpa up in a spare bedroom in the mansion of the starlet, where we can still see him getting by with his homely growth! The progenitor has small florets on spare heads, but it is history and if the shrub growth is contained by removing most of the suckers but retaining one or two, as I did today, it provides some interest to those of us who are probably quirky and know down deep that "beauty is still in the eye of the beholder" and that we don't have to hide Grandpa from general view. Mind, if you don't remove most of the suckers they will overcome your cultivar because the progenitor has as vigorous vegetative growth as its maker, Mother Nature. There is no harm in recognizing and prizing our origins, thick or thin and tough as nails!

Grass is a Plant

Sometimes it's hard to recall that grass is a plant when you see the beautifully cut carpet lawn of the North American golf course! The so-called lawn of the bucolic Lotus Island set is often the meadow grasses, cut to a higher measured level to retain uniformity. Taming the meadow grasses into a simulated lawn does not allow one to discard the recognition that one's grasses are a plant. As I have previously mentioned, we have two hundred varieties of grasses on the Pacific Coast and they vary greatly in growth habit. They are not, on the whole, all genetically engineered to flourish at half an inch or less. Neatness doesn't count, but sensitivity does if the free spirits of Mother Nature are allowed to flourish! I'm not suggesting for one minute that the fairway be cut to impede the ball from rolling. I'm not even suggesting the lawn-proud urbanite change his ways if the genetics of the turf are such that a half-inch set is a healthy thing. It's just that the heterogeneous grasses of Mother Nature will live together in perfect accord if you raise the bar a lot as you cut your so-called lawn. The grasses have been living together for centuries along with a mix of plants within the lawn on Lotus Island without a lot of outside help. The plants within the lawn are sometimes mistaken for green weeds by outsiders. The dominance of the composition of the so-called lawn varies from time to time depending on the changes in the climate. Celebrate that! Monoculture, as a general rule, in most instances leads to less adaptable outcomes. Mother Nature is wise! Aristotle said, "Nature does nothing in vain." Aristotle was also wise.

Bunnies and deer prefer mixed herbaceous food as well. Bunnies and deer are also wise. Celebrate that too! If we want to keep the ball rolling, limit monoculture to golf and lawn bowling.

Gunnera Attacked

It's fall, and the bucks of the black-tailed deer on Lotus Island, a subspecies of mule deer, are in rut! Whether they are getting rid of their antler velvet to get into fighting trim or practicing their moves against upcoming adversaries or both is moot. Either way, the young bucks are preparing for the coming conflict. Once the testosterone rises in deer or man, more activity will take place from the mid-brain. Whatever harm did my Gunnera plant do the bucks? And yet it is a convenient foil to attack: an inert adversary like a punching bag. The stems of Gunnera are coarse with rough spinous projections sufficiently sharp to remove the antler velvet. After that little favour by the plant, it's a short and unloving step to give the stems and leaves a good whacking with the newly hardened antlers. I've always said that Gunnera is a manly plant, so I suppose the deer feel it is a worthy opponent. The warrior class is simply doing what is necessary to perpetuate the species. Luckily for the gardener, the bucks are benign warriors throughout the growing year until fall, so the Gunnera enjoys a pristine existence until then. Actually, it is fortuitous that the rut begins in the fall, since it is nearly the end of the plant's season anyway, so it's a good way for the Gunnera to go out fighting. The plus for all this is that the bucks stop rubbing on the smaller ornamental trees which would otherwise be victimized. I hate the idea of surrounding all the little trees with wire cages. If you are not going to restrain the warrior class by fencing them out of your property, you must respect their need to train but hope that they will restrain themselves by confining their battle happily to the Gunnera, acting as the serendipitous stalking horse! That said, one gives thanks that young and fearless males are not wreaking havoc unselectively! If rut and heat went throughout the year the plant species would indeed be in jeopardy.

Penny for your Plots

On Monday my daughters and their partners came and planted the ailing elderly gentleman's dahlias in his time-established (in modesty I can't say honoured) protocol. In short, when the soil warms and the muck goes, an eight-inch-deep hole is dug every eighteen inches,* a handful of 13-16-10 is chucked in, and the Mantis tiller is jumped from hole to hole to make a soft feathery bed for the tuber. The dahlia root is chucked in on its soft little prepared bed, right side up, and a five-foot rebar is hammered in next to the tuber on its north side so we know the shoot will emerge south of the rebar when we first weed. The rebar is always on the north side of the tuber, which is covered with two inches of soil and lightly tamped. Later, the hole is hilled in as the sprouts grow and are gently tied to the rebar. My family planted over two hundred dahlias in this exemplary fashion.

One of the major faults of some large-flowered exhibition dahlias is weak flower stems. Large blooms with weak stems and the resultant floppy, droopy appearance is a big no-no! Out with those bulbs in the fall! Off with the flower heads in the summer! Some time ago the pianist noted that the cut bouquets of tulips she buys that droop become ramrod straight in the vase if a couple of copper pennies are placed in the water at the time of arrangement or later. I have, in the past, scoffed at her assertion, accusing her of magical thinking and avoiding recording p-values, but her repeated assessments in our living room, anecdotally at least, suggest penny energy might be real.

Unfortunately, I didn't think of pennies and her protocol in time to consider activating the technique into my current dahlia-planting scheme to cure floppy heads. There is nothing to lose. I may hold off on "out with the bulbs in the fall" for another year. I'll do penny for your plot next year if I am still here and lively. Another use for the dying Canadian penny! Chucking a few otherwise redundant pennies in the hole at the time of planting may be a cure for the weak stems of the more beautiful of the droopy dahlia varieties that are worth keeping but without favourable p-values I'm not holding my breath.

*Note: if you really want to be bothered exhibiting your dahlias, plant them three feet apart, not eighteen inches.

Winter Ducks

The Lotus Island harbour today, in early November, is teeming with American widgeons and bufflehead ducks! They come back to the same place in the harbour year after year and you could set your calendar by the day of their return. Vegetarians and carnivores! Dabbling ducks and diving ducks. They will be here all winter, sheltered in our little spot in the harbour to our great delight. The eagles have not returned yet to begin again with their connubial activity so the ducks have a short reprieve from danger. The buffleheads are much smaller than the widgeons, so are easier for the eagles to carry to their fledglings. The widgeons crowd serenely together, float along, seemingly unhurried, occasionally dabbling down when close to shore for plant food. They don't need to hurry because the plants wait for them. Their pace is unruffled. Why wouldn't it be? They are the gatherer society. When they dabble down, their little feathered arses stick straight up in the air. The little buffleheads skitter along, wings flapping repeatedly, posturing and diving and darting hither and yon! You can always identify them by the wake they leave; they move so fast with both feet and wings going a mile a minute in or on the water, chasing flesh! No wonder they are in a hurry. Their prey waits for no bufflehead so they have to be quick about it if they are to be a successful hunter society! The seagulls pester them, hoping they will drop the prey, but the buffleheads have an answer to that noisy and opportunistic feathered society. They swallow their prey underwater where no seagull will go. Then they emerge after they dive, well away from the gulls. They spend much of their time swimming around and through the widgeon flock so they give the appearance of hare, among tortoises. Curiously, the only winter ducks we usually see now are these two species. The harbour provides an abundant source of both plant and animal foodstuffs and the two species don't compete because of the nature of their respective diets. Aside from the eagles picking them off, their winter sojourn is untroubled. For the pianist and me, we could watch them all day; for us familiarity never breeds contempt!

Black Bamboo

In 1971 in Lotus City I combined several clumps of black bamboo (Phyllostachys nigra) along with Mexican fan palms and a tan-coloured aggregate of a pebble-like nature called Saturnalite. These materials were planted in a deep cleft in a rock hill. It appeared like a dry riverbed. Saturnalite is produced by heated and blown clay bodies to form a popcorn-like dry aggregate. It was quite beautiful, light and easy to work with, but had no nourishment for the plants. They required circumscribed soil deposited under the Saturnalite at each plant station. I wanted the bamboo to remain clumped and it did. My information at the time was that black bamboo was of a naturally clumping nature and would not spread. Since there had been an embargo on bamboo from China at around that time and particularly black bamboo, I was pleased to have it. I might have imagined I was in China as I sat daydreaming on my dry riverbed. Much later we moved from Lotus City to Lotus Island, both in the Pacific Northwest, and I took some rooted portions of the bamboo clumps with me. Lotus Island and Lotus City have winter temperatures that are at the top of cold tolerance for black bamboo, so the plants appreciate shelter. They are still in my garden on Lotus Island today, protected from ocean winds by the mixed windbreak hedges of Mother Nature. The black bamboo plantings weathered a particularly cold winter in 2010 with some top foliage loss. In the garden here, they are in three big clumps, but this year they have started to move! They have, for the first time in thirty years, begun to develop spreading rhizomes in spades! The clumps are monstrous and have probably responded to now-exhausted soil by seeking fertile land, sending probing rhizomes and creating new plants at a distance. When the bamboo was growing in Lotus City in the dry riverbed there was no nourishment from Saturnalite, so I provided water and fertilizer to the limited soil ball they lived on. There was no initiative on their part to look further on their own. They followed the adage, "Grow where you are planted." On the acreage of Lotus Island, even though clumping was their nature, they cast that aside and moved abroad, spreading and seeking new wealth when they had exhausted what they had for food in the old ground. Populations of anything, plant or animal, including human, do what they have to do, traveling to new ground, sacrificing their nature to survive and thrive. The alternatives are dependence, attrition, or death. It goes to show that the classification of clumping or spreading, in plant and animal, fails to account for the contingent capacity to change and move with whatever means necessary to survive! Climate and food trump sticking in the mud in the plant and animal world!

Regal Gooseberry Jam

Today I picked four pounds of dead ripe gooseberries from my bush—not rosy red, but the deeper purple-red colour of venous blood from a cyanosed patient! Picking gooseberries is hard work: avoiding the heavy thorns with a glove on the left hand to control the branch, picking selectively since the berries ripen to sweetness intermittently over a month. Even the dead ripe need a tug since the berries drop very late. I interim prune with the secateur as I pick, since the bush is huge and to get to its center without tearing your shirt or skin is the aim. Good pruning is necessary to get new wood to grow, as the berries are better on new wood than old. The gooseberry bush is next to a patch of red currants, which I now leave on the bushes as a stalking horse for the birds since red currants act as a magnet and mine contain currant maggot, protein for the birds. Mm mmm good. Since the skin of the gooseberry is tough and the armed branches are formidable, the birds leave them alone for an easier target.

I spent an hour or more after the pick today removing the occasional stem and the constantly present frass (my term for the withered remains of the flower). This is a tedious task. The next step was to freeze them in Ziplock bags for jam preparation. The freezing allows the juices to run more freely with cooking and require less water to be added. At jamming time the berries are softened in the microwave with enough water to minimally cover them and then they are mashed. Do not puree since the cooked berry skin is an essential feature of the jam. Sugar is added, equal parts, and cooked with the berry mash until the gel point or appropriate thickness approaches. If anyone thinks it is madness to go to all this work for a little jam, it is not. Gooseberry jam is a rare essence, not easily obtained, and is a high style of product, certainly ego-satisfying both to the purveyor and recipient. Since gooseberries are similar to the essential essence of people of a regal nature: tough-skinned, singular, and prickly as a gooseberry bush, it makes the work of those of us who choose to bring both berry and person and their potential sweetness and excellence to the fore, satisfying, since we labour in order to please and soften their hauteur. I love white bread and gooseberry jam, but sweet and piquant accompaniments to meat have also been tested and toasted over the centuries. Crabapple and chicken, applesauce and pork, cranberry and turkey, mint and lamb, Montmorency cherries and game—game and gooseberry, it rocks!

Quince Jelly

Two mature and knowledgeable ladies I know who like to make quince jelly took a large portion of my quince crop this past month, but I still had a number of these fruits that were hard to get rid of. Quince jelly is not for everyone! The flavour is rather unique. It has, however, an aromatic quality and a great deal more character than its cousins the apple and the pear, so I could not bring myself to discard the basket full of the fuzzy yellow fruit that was left behind after the ladies picked through it. I made my own quince jelly last week and it was very successful as the pectin content is high, even in the fully-ripened and over-ripened fruit that I used. Since quality jelly demands not only taste but colour and gel quality, my product will rate highly for the scarce aficionado who appreciates the unusual and less readily acquired flavour and appearance of quince jelly. The jelly in the jar has the colour of fine orange furniture oil, uniquely beautiful, to differentiate it from common red. I am also hoping that my value-added product will entice the extraordinarily wary who avoid the primary product, the fruit, but who could become new enthusiasts after trying the jelly. Those of low and undistinguished taste who require the more usual jellies on their toast can content themselves with the predictable. I do not intend to waste my time proselytizing any further to the un-adventuresome. You may think I am going clean overboard on this matter and you are probably right, as my position is not all that clean. I am one of the few on Lotus Island that has a fully productive quince tree (Cydonia oblonga) and pride and ego, I confess, has entered its ugly head as it gives me, I suppose, somewhat meager and pathetic bragging rights. I have no shame! I am sure there are more elderly eclectic ladies on Lotus Island that can be enticed with my jelly as I will allow it to speak for itself! As I was putting my jelly on the shelf, I heard a small sound from a jar. I listened carefully and think I heard it say, "Res ipsa loquitur, regards oblonga." ("I, the jelly, speak for myself.")

Identity, Our Tool is Us

It's fall today on Lotus Island and I cranked up my Bearcat shredder and munched and ground up my pile of pruned twigs and branches to pulp. I am old and feeble and have rheumatoid arthritis but with my tool as an extension of me, I am mighty! I am the Marlboro Man at work, employing a machine in a rugged activity that my forefathers, at my age, could have only dreamt about. I eventually ran out of gas at the same time as the Bearcat, so both of us called it a day. We all have tools that can be an extension of our arms or legs or brain or senses that make us explorers, visionaries, artists, and rugged adventurers! Whoever said, "It's not important what you do, but who you are" was not telling the whole story. We are creatures of our tools. In the olden days my father would watch my mother cut slices from the bread loaf. She exerted pressure, forcing the knife down heavily onto the loaf rather than deftly sawing with light downward force. She was always in a hurry. Her bread slices ended up crushed to about an inch high. My father would look at us and intone, "Let the tool do the work." Good advice! When the first primate, or the first crow, used the first tool to do a job that they had originally used an arm or beak to do, they began the process of advancing to a new identity that separated one from another. The artistry displayed by the operator of the excavator, who with foot and hand working together in harmonious accuracy can practically pick up a small pebble or lift a one-ton rock with his bucket, is astounding,. The machine has become a part of the body. With time and skill the tool incorporates into the organism so there is no space between the two. There becomes an area on the gyrus for the tool! Whether the golf club, the hockey stick, the brush, the egg whisk, the ivory keys, the strings, the cup, the pottery wheel, or the scalpel, when you have arrived at that golden moment when you are one with your tool, you will no longer see yourself apart from it!

Author

The author is a retired Orthopedic Surgeon who practiced surgery in Victoria, British Columbia for 45 years. He has lived on Salt Spring Island, British Columbia in a garden and orchard beside the water with his wife Joan, a ceramic artist and a pianist, for 30 years. They have celebrated 59 years together. He graduated from medicine at the University of Manitoba in 1957, obtained a M.Sc. in Anatomy in 1961 at the University of British Columbia and a Canadian Fellowship in Orthopedic Surgery in 1963. The role of the garden has given him the blessing of exultation and serenity that he drew on to meet the pressures of his surgical practice and responsibilities to impart the joy of gardening and understanding to his children and grandchildren and to encourage the love of nature and the environment. He has published two books in the past with Friesen Press, *An Elderly Eclectic Gentleman* and *A Braided Cord*. He writes from time to time in a blog on the Web Site:

www.jimwarren.ca

Thanks to David Kasper
for the cover photograph of Sunrise over the Salish Sea.

Printed in Canada